DEC 18, 2011

To: EVELYN
THANK YOU FOR
YOUR KIND, CARING
WAY AND SHARING
YOUR LIGHT SO
FREELY, WITH EASE.

Love,
& Frieda
XO

THE LEGENDS OF NOW

A Love Anthology

FRIEDA LIVESEY

Library and Archives Canada Cataloguing in Publication
Livesey, Frieda, 1947– The legends of NOW : a love anthology / Frieda Livesey.

I. Title.

PW8623.I9235L44 2009   C818'.6   C2009-905625-9

Editing by David F. Rooney
Proofreading by Ann Harmer
Book design by Fiona Raven
Front cover artwork by Rachel A. Kelly
Photo of front cover artwork by David F. Rooney
Story illustrations by Sarah Golden
Automatic drawings by Mieke Blommestein and Frieda Livesey
Photos of automatic drawings by David F. Rooney
Goal setting coaching by Tony Collins
Author photo by Jason Keerak

www.TheLegendsOfNow.com

Published by:

FriesenPress

Suite 300 – 852 Fort Street
Victoria, BC, Canada V8W 1H8

www.friesenpress.com

Distributed to the trade by The Ingram Book Company

*I dedicate this book
to the inestimable Grace
of the whole human race
that assists me NOW
as I AM,
unfolding—
endlessly.*

Contents

Introduction

From the authentic vibe of life's All-As-One Tribe
Love brings forth these writings so true

Straight arrows of blue
For ALL, me and you

ALL we know—we are NOW
As one Great Holy Cow

As our fates will allow
We let go of the plow

Together we flow
Love's soft lightness glow

Remembering our way
We start NOW to say

"We're ALIVE!"

Thank You

I send a thank you to all source lights that have deeply sparked creative inspiration within my heart to write and to capture the essence of beauty's diverse song, so naturally singing for all to hear, beyond words.

*"In rivers, the water you touch
is the last of what has passed
and the first of that which comes;
so with time present."*

—LEONARDO DA VINCI

Automatic Drawings and Written Guidance

Automatic Drawing and Writing is the practice of allowing spirit to control the writing hand, to convey drawings and/or written guidance.

Focus, relaxation and overcoming apprehension are essential in automatic drawing or writing. When a guide takes over and begins to write, it is a very harmonious relationship, one that is connected and flowing from both sides. The focus is on *allowing* the pen to write without concern for what it *should* write. Automatic writing is not about focusing on the words; it is about allowing the action. Some artists use similar methods in various mediums, focusing on gently allowing creative expression to flow through naturally.

My dear friend Mieke Blommestein has facilitated many confirming automatic drawings and written guidance over the past several years. Mieke has been practicing automatic drawing and writing for more than twenty years. When she and I put our hands together and engage in automatic drawing, I have a uniquely deep inner understanding of these drawings as a direct knowing from within. These drawings have assisted me step by step to trust the pure intention of source energy and the divine purpose of all vibration that is expanding consciousness here and now.

I have included photos of two automatic drawings and their writings; these are communications from two of my main guides.

The first automatic drawing and guidance is from my dad, who passed over on September 22, 1990. Dad is my main guide and has never ceased to confirm my daily process of expansion through inspiring insights, deep inner understandings and pure love.

In this drawing and writing, Dad comes through to state, *"You are now connected to your children because you now have a better understanding of life. As I filled up my baskets of flowers, I kept myself busy and I forgot what life was all about."* You see in the drawing that my children are inside my pockets.

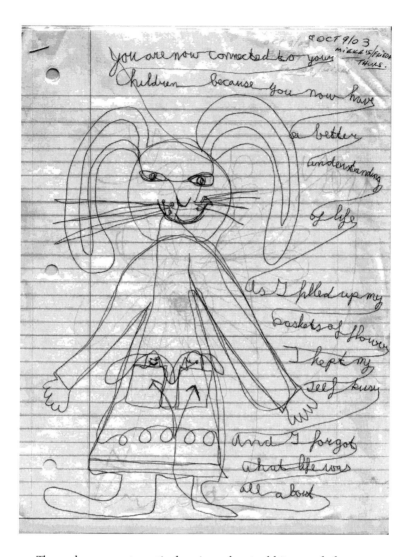

Through many automatic drawings about rabbits, my dad came through to describe my progress along the path of light and love that I have intended. In the beginning, I was a scared rabbit in a cage of my own creation. Then I was in a cage with the door open, but I was still not coming out. Later I was out on the grass beside the cage. Finally I was a rabbit in motion, hopping around happily up and down.

The second automatic drawing and guidance is from my driving guide, Dominique. In this drawing, Dominique states, *"My name is Dominique. I am your guide as well. I loved history as well as you did. I am with you when you drive your car."* This drawing was such a confirmation, as I knew there was a loving presence with me when I drove the car.

My first encounter with Dominique was on a foggy and snowy drive home from Kelowna, BC, to Revelstoke, BC in the dark. I was leaning over the steering wheel, straining for a better view and wishing I could see farther along the highway. All of a sudden, Dominique conveyed this understanding, beyond words: *"You will always be able to see far enough to move ahead along your path and then, from there, you will be able to see ahead again."* I slumped back into the driver's seat and relaxed, knowing and feeling the truth of this within my being.

Experiencing the natural nature of this unique loving guidance, through automatic drawings and writings, has helped me let go of some deeply held fear patterns about life circumstances by coming to understand and trust that constant universal love and inner guidance are so near at hand. Through focused intention, I can tune into this guidance, to request and receive unlimited assistance.

A Story for Sarah

White Goose was leading her goslings down to the pond near her home, when she got her foot tangled in the underbrush. She squawked and honked and hooted until a passing coyote heard her calls and came to investigate the racket. The noise sounded to him like a goose, and yet it seemed to sound like a chicken and owl as well. Coyote hesitated, listened more closely, then strode forward to see for himself what type of bird was in distress.

Now, White Goose was no ordinary goose. She was very unique! She was the kind of bird who rarely did what was expected of her. She walked her own walk and she talked her own talk. And she taught her goslings to do the same. She knew her name well and it was not Go-Along-With-The-Crowd. It was Pay-Attention-To-What-You-Want. White Goose knew she needed to call loudly for help, and so she did, in every possible way that she could. Her goslings heard her loud, alarming calls and hid in the undergrowth.

Coyote approached the goose cautiously, looking left and right, then up and down along the path. He had never heard such strange sounds coming from a goose. He looked more closely to make certain it actually was a goose and could clearly see it was! "Why the strange calls?" asked the coyote.

"Strange!" said goose. "There is nothing at all strange about my calls. I am caught and require assistance. This is my unique way of asking, in no uncertain terms, for exactly what I require. If I had not expressed the depth of my true feelings, you may not have responded as you did."

"Your unusual cries did make me very curious," said coyote. "I felt a strong need to see for myself where these sounds came from."

"Thank you for coming!" said goose. "Would you please try and untangle my foot? My goslings are waiting for me under those bushes over there."

"Of course," said coyote "What's in it for me?"

"You will see," said goose "You will see. Trust me." So coyote gnawed the tangle of roots off White Goose's leg, and soon she was fancy-free and waddling along the path towards her goslings, who ran out to greet her.

Coyote said, "Wait a minute! You said I would see what was in this for me!"

"You will," said goose, without giving it another thought. "It is beyond words that the worth of a deed, well done, appears. Be patient with yourself and in a moment, you will understand the goodness of your actions. You will see it in the kindness others show to you, just as you have been kind to me. You will see it in the way you now know more about who you are. You will see it in the brilliance of each shining star you begin to see. You are a knower and in your deepest knowing, you will see the worth of your kind deeds. Payback comes in unexpected ways and makes your days shine like diamonds and gold. Trust me and you will see. All is well, coyote, all is well."

Coyote loved the sound of what goose was saying. He knew she was not really a silly goose as he had first thought, for he sensed the wisdom of her words. He decided to make a new start. He decided to trust the goose and to stay loose like a goose and to know, in his smart-heart, all would be well.

A story of Truth

Once upon a time, in the heart of Africa, lived a giraffe named Fred. Fred was fearful. He didn't know why this was, but his angels did. Fred had more angels than you could shake a stick at, but he found it difficult to believe he had even one. His guides and angels never gave up on him—not once!

Fred did know of the stories and the pictures from The Book of Life that the angels read aloud. He just wasn't certain of the source and this uncertainty confused him.

"Why do I seem different?" mused Fred. "I don't want to be different. I won't fit in the forest if I am." Fred sometimes would admit to himself that he knew what he truly knew and sometimes he would just see what he wanted to see to feel accepted in the forest.

One day, while Fred was sleeping, the green fairy-angel of Africa's great heart decided to open up Fred's Book of Life to an old page where dragons and leprechauns danced and spiders wove stories for all. This old passage showed Fred his endless, universal connections. Fred stirred within. He remembered the warm glow of the connecting force of all and his clear view of himself, naturally with all, softened. His heart felt like happy jelly and it started to sing: "I'm looking over a four-leaf clover, that I overlooked before." It made Fred want to dance in the meadow and across the plains with all of his friends.

"I remember," said Fred. "I remember our source. It is gently-powerful and warm. It never judges or leaves us. We are never alone." Fred's heart grew in every direction that day and he accepted himself into it, knowing that he could hold everything in his heart and never fear losing connection with any of the life he loved.

And so it is, to this day, that giraffes naturally stand firmly on the ground with all four feet and yet maintain a constant clear view of truth above the clouds.

Alfred Alligator

Alfred Alligator ventured forth into the swamp one day to play the play of life he knows so well. In the eternal wellness of all that is, endless day into night, he spliced his way into this scene of endless scenes that he lives in most of the time. The sets in his scene were so familiar. He had explored and expanded himself around most of these scenes—seeing, tasting, hearing, smelling and sensing everything high and low. In the sun and in the rain, in the clouds and during bright, clear open-skied reflections, Alfred explored. Alfred was witness to the bottom and the top of this swamp and all of its uneven edges.

The patterns of the swamp grass caused Alfred to yawn and relax within. The airy mosses draping lazily down from the swamp trees gave a feathery-soft texture to the view Alfred loved. This swamp felt like Alfred's space of all eternal spaces.

Alfred's brothers, sisters and extended family played nearby. Alfred Alligator had only one note of discontent in his vibratory being. Alfred was not seeing the light of his life lately. He was living in the edginess of not knowing his growth of becoming more, and that was very unusual for him. Alfred was not a shy guy most of the time. He was social and playful and full of fun.

Lately, Alfred had been spending a lot of time in the bottom of the swamp, sorting things out for himself. It was cool down there and the mud felt so good on his leathery alligator skin. The mud soothed Alfred to smoothness, which brought him to a deep appreciation of this scene of all scenes that he called home. Just as Alfred was finishing his mud bath, he started to laugh. He realized that he had been thinking too hard again and his thinker was sore. Alfred knew that when this happened, he could not see his inner light. He swore he would spend more time in the mud. Somehow mud bathing helped his blood to flow more smoothly and then Alfred could, naturally, return again to knowing the light of his life.

All Is Well

A wellspring of hope, within me rises up
Upon its own in-dwelling
To reveal itself in lightness and love
So refined, it is undefined
Or indefinable.

Creating a word may seem quite absurd,
Yet the language does flow from its
Own usage upon itself
And X marks the spot of a
Man that does not understand his own sign,
That is wholly divine.

Blue ink on a page
That ripens with age
To a vintage; refined,
And a language so kind
That *One of a kind* will
remind the whole mass
Not to be crass to itself.

For the stuff of an elf,
Expressing itself,
Will show in the glow,
A flicker, a flow,
To enhance all to know
Of mankind.

Angels

Angels are a part of me
They help with everything I see
The beauty-flow within my heart
Reflects the love that is

Angels in us one and all
Their wings have feathers small and tall
Although we think them far away
Our angels touch us now

I see the angel that you are
Connecting hearts are never far
You've taught me much of grace and ease
And bless me with your smile

Thank you for the love you share
The easy open way you care
You always know the words to say
And love me as I am

Bless This Man

Beyond a garden wall, a man sits and waits for the tears to pass.
He is in a winter and frozen emotions.
Summer will find him soon and melt his heart.
The flowers surrounding him will bloom.
He will be free to enjoy wholeness.
Bless this man for all that he has learned by his own hand.
His experience has healed us all.
Lessons come in unlimited ways.
Knowing how not to live life is a valuable lesson.

Central Sun

Beyond the mind's understanding, the heart fulfills its obligation to absolute unity. Let it go, let it go, let it all go, and all of the world-weary observations will melt away like butter on a hot day.

Allow the truth of lightness to find you fully. Hold your head high and stand in the sun that shines, within, beyond our sun. This sun has the healing rays of all love. This sun has a message for the world. This message is a new vibration. The wind will assist this message to establish a new rhythm.

A new chorus will rise up from this and the singing will heal all views. Love awaits you in your spacious open-hearted view. Accept yourself fully. You are the light. As you accept this, step by step, a new understanding of love alone will rise up in your bosom. You will understand your own shining to a greater degree and thus, this newly acquired understanding will go out to others of its own accord.

Give yourself credit for your heart-understanding. Open your heart to yourself completely without protective thought. Life is love and needs no protection. The mind will move aside as the heart understands. Keep this self-kindness close beside you to understand what self-kindness is. You may see what it is *not* first and then clarity will assist your view.

Maintain your own, unique vibration at all times with self-kindness and self-love. There is no resistance here, just a deep, knowing view regarding your absolute worthiness. Through this, you will see your inner strength. The strength of *all-heart* will fill your being and you will be gentle-strength personified; send this universal strength of love alone out from the source extension you intrinsically are.

You are a vessel for love. This is not the faint-of-heart love of narrow worldly understandings but an all-inclusive package deal that all have access to—everlasting love. The head will ask, "What is this?"

The heart will remember its innocent origins and rejoice in being light-hearted again.

You bear the key to your own kingdom of peace from within, my child. No other can give this to you. Trust your own innate wisdom and say to yourself often, "All is well, as it is," to see wellness clearly in your heart with your knowing inner eye.

Bowing

Spendthrifts bow to the miserly creed
Blessings bow to every misdeed
Honour bows to holding your own
As hanging up bows to holding the phone
Beside yourself bows to welcome within
Judgment bows to there is no sin
Spying bows to what will life bring?
Deafness bows to hear the bell ring!
Hesitance bows to bringing love home
Blindness bows to sight in the bone
Sideways bows to centered within
While "special" bows to the all you have been
Meandering bows to steady and strong
A tall elf bows to life and belong
Static bows to stasis and growth
Mercantile bows to one seamless loaf
Aristocrat bows to the peasant in all
Angel wing bows to naturally tall
Blissing-out bows to a steadying gaze
Low voltage bows to the effortless phase
Glue and all stickiness bow to adhere
Foggy and faded out bow to all clear
Missing in action bows to the brave
Because lingering attachment bows to behave
Leaving and zoning out bow to right here
When abandonment bows to accepting what's clear
Questions and answering bow to behold
Searching and seeking out bow to enfold

In the honour we stand in, the light comes to see
The mission of missions is built into me.
The stone that I stand on steadies my foot
In the now of expansion, just as it's put.
Light, in its wisdom, is coming again
To the theatre near All, hear the refrain!

Faith

Hold tight to your faith by simply remaining in it. Do not sabotage yourself by abandoning yourself. Faith is what you are. You do not have to hold your nose at a particular angle, light twelve candles, burn incense, etc., unless it helps you to stay in faith in some way. These things may be skillful means for you to remain in faith, but they are not necessary to faith's presence in you.

Connect, connect, connect, and the practice of connection will make being faith second nature to your heart. Little by little, self-abandonment will become an old, forgotten memory. Trust yourself to know, fully, what the next right step for you is. Encourage others to trust themselves as well. Self-trust is an old understanding called common sense, which was never so very common.

Now the trust required is deeper and more complete. Lift your own heart by trusting it completely. There is magic in self-trust, the kind of magic you cannot find anywhere else. This kind of magic creates love in your life and thus in the lives of others. Trust your intuition and your subtle senses to lead you through your days. Say goodbye to fear as an old form of protection that never really protected you at all, but actually added to your predicament. Laugh as you realize this. It is pretty funny how the mind rationalizes fear and then keeps up a steady patter to justify its existence. This is part of our lesson together here on this earth plane—to overcome fear and to recognize, fully, the absolute strength of the heart muscle. Exercise alone is not what strengthens the heart muscle. Self-acceptance and self-love do.

With a strong heart, your eyes will see in a new way and your ears will hear more clearly. Your skin will be more vibrant and your knees will have more flexibility. All this from self-acceptance? you ask. More, so much more, will flow with your open heart. Feel life and let it go. Love is a flow in the universe and you are too. You are a flow of power, trust, faith, hope, discernment, creativity, compassion and love.

Universal love includes everything. Are you not alive and part of life? Sing with the singers or sew with the sewers. Dance with the dancers or crow with the crowers. It does not matter what you do. It is in the being that you remain present in life and it is in the being that all of the magical properties of abundance are in you and you are them. Have faith in this knowing and in your capability to be present for yourself. You are a gift to yourself and the universe. Accept that gift you are and be love. No harm will come to you in this lifetime for being faith. In faith you will naturally know all is well.

Feelings

I feel such subtle feelings today. I feel feelings of the
heart. The heart is calling. I know her so well.
I miss her voice. What do I feel? I feel I am a
warrior that is so tired. I feel the illusion of my
battles and I am ready to step back, into love, and
lay my weapons down. I feel foolish for admitting
my frailty. I feel ashamed for being a burden. I
feel at a loss for words to describe this subtle,
yet strong, knowing that is coming more and more.
I feel alive in a new way and a subtle uncertainty
here, in this opening space. I feel alone and unworthy of
recognition that has come unbidden. I feel unable
to receive, fully receive, all that is mine by
birth, by creation, by design. Feelings are a
flow within me and I am exploring my expression of them. I am
surrendering, surrendering, surrendering any resistance to feel.
The subtle sense of all as truth is arriving in my
view.

I am love as I am focused in love. I am lost as I am focused in
fear. It is like standing on the border between
Saskatchewan and Manitoba and stepping back and
forth. I am in Saskatchewan. I am in Manitoba—
Saskatchewan, Manitoba. I feel subtle clarity and
joy within and fear is coming up for inclusion in
love. I feel pondering, wavering, aligning and finding my
feet on the "sunny side of the street." The softer
view of love of my manifestation is here and I welcome it
whole-heartedly. I also feel welcoming of my strong will
as a provider for truth and not a defendant of old
inner trials.

The war is over within me and I am surveying, with assistance, the debris of the aftermath in a universal relief camp, where all exist and none are excluded. It is an infinite relief camp with many unique expressions in it, and I am healing my view here in this spacious understanding of all as one love. I feel safety and belonging here. I do not feel fear or any other reaction viewing this place of surrender. My lack of reaction surprises and comforts my heart. I feel all are united and healing together. I feel relief and release, but most of all, I feel detachment from the ancient war within. I see the strong loving feeling that I am, teaching and guiding me.

I am life, feeling oneness. I am life, feeling well. I am life, feeling alive.
I simply allow feeling the love of life I am in all ways. The dogs of war are gone now and
I am feeling. I am curiously feeling and healing my view.

Is

A new understanding evolves and yet, beyond the wonder and disbelief lies an old remembering of a balance and a harmony that just eternally *is*. Is it not the things that we feel so certain of that we take for granted and forget the harmony of receiving and giving in the natural order of peaceful flow? The subtle daily guidance we receive simply *is*. It is as soft as a kitten's whisker and as fine as a silken laugh from the lips of a child.

The universal order of our lives will not change. We will still live and laugh and learn, but we will hold ourselves more gently, as we sense ourselves being held in love. We will hear ourselves more clearly as we know we are heard by larger, more compassionate ears. We will talk to ourselves with a gentler voice as we are told, with love, the story of our original nature. We will flow with gratitude as we sense the flow of all around us that holds us in the arms of gentle truth.

Our unique obstacles are not the obstacles of others. As we see being loved completely, obstacles and all, we will find the capacity to fully open our hearts to our humanity, our connection to all in the same boat, on the high sea of eternal-life school.

"Row, row, row your boat, gently down the stream. Merrily, merrily, merrily, merrily, life is but a dream."

Life-Flow

The grand design is so divine
Right from the hip and free design
A designation from before
An open door to Evermore

And still the lacy spectral tie
A loose rappel and eagle's eye
No self-containing, keeping score
Straight from the attic to the floor

Oh, floribunda, look at you
Swimming freely in this stew
With all the pieces full and fit
A fruit and flower from the pit

I hasten to throw you a kiss
A straight white arrow, not a miss
You are the star I dreamt of then
I see you rising once again

A storm of plenty starts to pour
And no one now is keeping score
No truer lantern from the core
To light the way to Evermore

Love Alone

Sing the song of love and plenty, overriding lack and less
Hold the dancer to your bosom, send the music out to bless
Kisses hold us like an anchor, softly planted, wholly meant
In the dark of every passage, keep your head forever bent

Mark this song with gales of laughter, sift it slowly in the wind
Hear the chorus call you forward, knowing all that you have been
Song of love and song of freedom, stiff and sparkling all in one
Hold my hand and flow with silence, in the brilliance of the sun

Candles weeping, overflowing, setting free a pool of tears
Sending ripples through the cosmos, lighting pathways through
    the years
Heavy holdings, long forgotten, rising up and floating free
Lifting up the hearts of many, flowing clear for all to see

In the beauty of the morning, read the love upon your face
Serve the souls so lost beside you, find some comfort in their place
We are one with all who love us, flowing ever to our source
Guided by the lights of love, to keep a steady, sturdy course

Thank you, thank you, every singer, small and tall and in-between
You have given love new meaning, never fearing to be seen
Vibrance of the world in focus, resting, being all it can
Feeling heartbeat of a love song, backed up by a healing band

Choose your life and choose your living, make your choices from
    your heart
Any age and any vision, never is it late to start
Cast your net and bring in fishes, know they nourish self and all
New beliefs of life to live in, moving forward, walking tall

Inner Truce

The wind swept the plains. The animals residing there knew well of the winds that blew in their lives. They hunkered down with their backs against the wind and patiently waited it out. Their animal instincts told them that the wind would calm again. They understood that the wind is not their constancy of experience.

The willow, at the water's edge, bowed her head in knowing grace and flowed with the wind's blustery way. She knew the wind well. Her roots were deep in the waters of life and this depth sustained her in the winds of change blowing her life around. She stood firm yet flexible and waved her willowy branches in the breezes that blew her to a deeper understanding of her naturally rooted strength from within.

The lemon tree did not fare so well in the wind. It had shallow roots and was uprooted easily and often in the winds of time. This did not upset the lemon tree. Hers was a natural knowing of the way of beginning again from scratch. She taught this lesson to all on her path over and over again. She endlessly began again with ease. The lemon tree knew this depth of structure well and trusted re-rooting deeply from her own, unique experiencing.

The robin sang a song of love and flew with the winds of change. She loved the wind so much. She played in it. She frolicked up and down, feeling the wind in her feathery features. The robin felt absolutely refreshed by the wind. She blessed the wind's passage in her life and all that went with it. The robin understood that the wind supported her wings in flight. She relaxed and enjoyed the ride of the highs and lows that the winds of change brought in the moment of its creative capability.

That beast of burden, the donkey, hated the winds of change no matter how little or how expansively they blew. He felt the wind added to his burden and blew sand into his eyes, so he could not see clearly to move his large loads forward, up the path of life. His was a unique view as well and taught him and all around him patience and acceptance of burden-consciousness as a groundswell understanding.

The sheep also had a unique view of the wind. The sheep paid close attention to all movement around him. He moved intrinsically with all. He moved from his gut instincts. The sheep knew in his heart to move with the tribe, beyond bribery, to survive and to even thrive in the here and now. The sheep let his fleece go in the winds of change.

The wind of change knows itself in the unlimited diversity of nature's expression, experiencing light-evolution on earth.

Let the wind blow, let the body glow in the knowing of all is well, from within. The stage of the endless staging of life calls us all forward, uniquely, to play our part in the art of making love here and now. The plow of diversity—plowing the field of dreams into a dream team—is aligning us all as one lovely universal dream expanding all love of life. This expanding view lives in all life, all ways, all of the time. This whole view is called Now.

Let the wind in. Let new life begin. Feel the refreshment past the din of win-or-lose, or snoozing's way of not being present, to be the gift of life you are. Play the starring role in your own life.

A point of illumination is the point of wind. Steady your sails. Point yourself into the wind. Allow the gales to pass and ask yourself, "Who am I now?" Then know, from within, "I am the wind of change and the changeling in the wind, embracing me now. I naturally honour the duality that I am. I am willing to be me, right here and now. I fully live my life as my willing life fully lives me."

The Rabbit and the Python

The Python is a snake of wonder and vast imaginings. It has the strength of a lion, and yet it has no cunning. It is driven by a deep sense of belonging in the all. In this way, it is innocence personified. The rabbit holds great fear of the python. Rabbit's fear is passed down from generations of rabbits who have seen their kin eaten whole by python. Eating prey is not personal to python. He is hungry and rabbit is his prey. To rabbit, however, it is a little personal. Fear is held and a hypervigilant view is maintained when anything that smells, moves or sounds like python appears.

Mother rabbit saw grass move in the distance. She became agitated and fearful. Her senses became heightened and with this, she became edgy and on high alert. Just then, her little one leapt on her from a nearby rock and she overreacted so much that her heart stopped. She lay panting, unable to tend to her brood. In a moment or two of quietude, rabbit regained her focus and her watching post.

The rippling grass came very near, and as mother rabbit strained to see, she saw clearly that this movement was not python at all. It was lizard. Lizard was harmless. Rabbit had injured herself in her fear-of-death view that she had accepted. Rabbit had no personal experience of python. This view was something she carried as an old consciousness, handed down. She was about to let it go.

Lizard stopped to visit. He saw rabbit's fear-face and said, "Rabbit, why are you so fearful?"

Rabbit said, "I was watching the grass rippling as you approached and I remembered stories the elders told of python that I imagined as just this ripple." Lizard laughed kindly.

"These are very old stories, rabbit. Look around you. Have you or your family ever actually seen a python?"

"No," said rabbit. "There have been no pythons in this location for hundreds of years."

"You have no need to fear python anyway, rabbit. If it is your turn to be eaten, you will be eaten. It is not personal. Do everything you can do to protect your family and home, but then relax and enjoy your living. You are killing yourself, my friend. Is that not funny?"

"I see what you mean," said rabbit. "I have trained my mind to see crisis everywhere and I find it so hard to relax and flow with the natural stream of living."

"That's it!" said lizard. "You can do it! Give it a try!"

"I will," said rabbit. "I will. I live in a beautiful home in the grasslands. I have food and water and beautiful, bouncy bunnies. I will remember how good life is and I will let go of crisis. I will allow life to flow through me to all."

As fate would have it, one day python was crossing this meadow to get to the other side. He was full of zebra and he needed to find a tall tree to sleep in. He was so sleepy. In the middle of the meadow, rabbit met python, but she didn't know who he was, so she was not afraid. She stopped to talk. Python wasn't very chatty, as he was so sleepy, but he managed a "howdy do," and off he went to find his tree.

In the morning, the lizard returned to visit rabbit. On his way, he saw the python hanging out in the tall tree on the field's edge. "Oh, no!" he thought as he hurried off to check on rabbit, for he had seen python before. After lizard explained what python looked like, rabbit was amazed. She remembered how python had actually been. He wasn't at all like the elders had remembered him. He wasn't mean to her or her little ones. He was focused on getting on, for sure, but he was polite enough.

"It wasn't your time to die," said lizard. "It was your time to live and experience life. When it is your time to die, dying will occur. Until then, don't worry."

"I'm so glad I had that experience with python," said rabbit. "Now I can pass on, from my own experience, what I have observed about python and not this old death-fear that was told to me."

Lizard left rabbit and her family. He knew rabbit understood a deeper meaning of life now, beyond fear. He saw the sense of wonder in rabbit's sparkly eyes. He felt her conviction and inner strength to fully live her life. He felt certain that she could now cope with any scenario presenting itself and not stop her own heart from beating, even if it was her time to die. He knew rabbit would enjoy her life in the abundance of the forest that she lived in and she would teach others, from her own solidly understood experience, that fear has no power over you unless you give it power from your mind.

Python and rabbit lived for years side-by-side in harmony. They crossed each other's path at times and respected each other's expression. Rabbit died of old age. She had no fear, and so she refused to kill herself by creating it. She knew there was more than enough abundance in this field for all that inhabited it. She saw how this is. Lizard had helped her see how to love her life fearlessly.

Marvel

Spacious creators and singers of song
Moods in the backsweep that help us along
Florals and prints and oh, indigo blue
All the creations of me and of you

Sentences, hearings and trials of the heart
Moving through passages, playing our part
Letting the icicles drip from our chin
These are the memories of where we have been

Creatures of habit and solace and fright
Sinking in septic tanks, calling it might
Letting revival release all we own
Walking our given path all the way home

Kin of the forest and shine of the stars
Can we now see that what is, is all ours
Kept in the closet for so many years
Out in an instant and dragged by all ears

Here's to the wholeness in all that resides
Hearts in the neighborhood, movers of tides
Is there a name for the beauty we are
Let's just condense it and call it a star

Rejoice when we're absent, rejoice when we're blessed
Rejoice when we find we are doing our best
It's not in the judging we better our breed
It's in our remembering to listen and heed

The Bee All

A bee flew by to share a view
A bee of colour, a bee of hue
A bee of brightness, of shining gold
A forever-bee, or so I'm told

She stopped, she started and then stood still
She waited for clarity high on a hill
She talked of forgiveness, then set herself free
So she could relate to you and to me

This bee of the high road is here by day
By night, you will find her far away
Her song is the same wherever she goes
Her song is her freedom and all that she knows

Her tale is of trials and struggles and fright
Her tools are her longings of wrongs made right
Together with all bees, she's safe in the hive
Togetherness always makes her feel alive

The honey of plenty, of always, of now
The honey of Krishna, of Jesus, of Tao
Remembered in buzzing from flower to flower
Remembered in living free hour to hour
Bee free!

A Story of Unification through Diversity

In a land not far from here, there lived a star. He was a very bright, luminous star, but he did not know the beauty of his own lightness. Many people told this star of his brightness, but he would respond with, "Thank you!" or "That's nice." In fact, the star could not accept his bright visage. The night would pass, the day would come and the star would say, "What's it all about?" This subtle questioning was a gentle, inner asking, for the star earnestly wanted understanding of his shining. The star did not yet know that all he had to do was believe. That was it! He just had to believe in his own star power and he would have all of the understanding required.

The magic of belief escaped the star until one day at twilight he saw his full brightness reflected in the ocean's surface. There was no one anywhere near him, so he knew it must be he who was so clearly reflected in this living mirror. The sturdy little star was speechless, staring at the skinny spikes of light emanating around his reflection. He looked away and looked back again, thinking he may have wanted to see this so badly that he had imagined it, but the sparkling reflection of his presence was still there. It was blue and white and silver, with sparks of deep purple in the depths of the shine. He felt grateful for this opportunity to see himself more clearly. He said, "Thank you!" to whoever might be listening. He said this from a very certain part of himself. He said this without words. He knew he meant this thank you deeply. A response returned from the depth of the sea. It was not the kind of response you would make up to impress or coerce your mind. It was a mystical response that returned naturally, and it filled the star with satisfaction.

The reply was a wave so big that it wrapped itself high over the giant black rocks on the ocean's edge. As the wave subsided, the star saw its point of illumination was still there, shining like a bright beacon in the ocean's mirror. After the wave had passed, the ocean was still and reflected only light and love on its lovely, fluid surface. The star knew who he was with prismatic clarity beyond all clear and present danger. The star recognized his face in the peaceful reflection of the continuum of now, unfolding in silence and absolute stillness. Nothing changed about the star. He didn't become prideful or arrogant. In this deep self-knowledge, the star saw that all life is continually becoming. He saw the beauty of all as a colourful light patterning. This settled the star to complete self-acceptance. Life made sense to the star's heart-song. He saw the perfect order of all life and that he was an intrinsic part of this artistry. He saw that this beauty he is never ceased to expand itself.

The star said, "May the weather come and go. May the winds blow and blow. I will know. I will know that truth is the beautiful mystery of all for one and one for all. The call of the wild knows this well."

In the silence, the star had found the answer to a question he had asked himself for so very long. Who am I?

The answer came back on the lips of the wind: "You are the wind of a thousand winds, the eye of a thousand eyes and the voice of every voice voicing. You are one with all life."

The star's understanding grew with each expanding moment and he perceived with a clarity he had never even considered. Birds sang in the light he shone. He knew his was the light of all shining and he gave thanks for this understanding. He gave thanks for everything as it is and especially for the diversity within the unification of all.

Walk through *any* door and find love alone

Find it in the wind and in your sleeping
Find it in your breath and in your weeping
See it in the sigh of every passing wave
See it in the sign on every stalwart grave
Know it in the song that passes in the night
Know it in the smile that could have been a fight
Feel it in the flow of every passing day
Feel it in your palms and shoulders as you pray
Sense it in the grasses flowing in the breeze
Sense it in each flower that puts your mind at ease
Allow it in the sun that holds you in its gaze
Allow it in the peace of seeing bygone days
Arrive to find the love that you had sent before
Arrive to love's surprise, here, waiting at your door
Is it a surprise with all this love you feel?
Is it just a dream or are you getting real?
Every passing note that holds you in the song
Every passing change, no rightness and no wrong
Leads you to belief that life is just a song
Leads you to this space where you can sing along
Even in the mist, you knew there was a way
Even in the dark, you tried so hard to play
Every daisy knows its petals rise and fall
Every light within reminds us to stand tall
Flowers in a field invite you to expand
Flowers in your heart are flowers in your hand
Take the life you own and open every door
Take the time to see all love and you are more
Angels hold your hand and walk with you awhile
Angels hold your heart in every knowing smile
After being cold, the fire is nice to see

After being lost, it's better to be me
Actions are the words that carry forth the love
Actions are the service of every peace-filled dove
Is it a surprise to see the love come in?
Is it a surprise to sense it with a grin?
See the water rise and let it softly flood
See the ocean cleanse and feel it in your blood
Every fairy's flight assists us to go home
Every faith and trust can take us to the zone
Know you are the door to all that's gone before
Know your heart, the lantern, and light it from your core
Express the utter magic and let the music flow
Express your open heart as you learn to let go
Ask your soul for guidance, then raise your eyes to see
Ask for gentle lifting up to know that you can be

Amplify soul messages through integration and letting go of old, noisy habits of self-protective thought

Carry every laden thought to the grave of misrepresentation and let it go. Allow the light of love to shine within you and let it shine out from you for all to see. The beauty of our inner selves is our true beauty. It is our spiritual stature and our song of deliverance from old troubles and inner pains. Flow with this river of life that you fully feel within you. Let life move in its own miraculous way. Do not hold yourself in bondage for the rigors of any illusive set of rules that no longer applies to your heart and soul. Set yourself free to be love. Speak from your basis of all understanding. March to the drum that you hear so clearly. Lift your legs high and place your feet forward. Ready, set, go.

The lion and the butterfly have equal strength, but it is in their own, unique, expression that this strength is shown. There is no need for protection of any kind—no need for comparison or competition.

Let it all go—all, every.

Let every fiber, cell nucleus and DNA strand resonate with this love that is. Know your love is all love and all other's love is your love. Share from your heart without protection or holding back.

Slices of life recall a bigger blanket, a larger flow. Be still. Sit in the sun. Know you are one with all. Steady yourself when you feel old patterns rise and hold your heart near saying: All is well, all is well. We are one with all soul-lit hearts.

Consider the fish of a different pond. Do they swim in the same way? Their energy touches all others, too. Environment is a huge word that encompasses us all in every facet and every freedom.

Open up your heart to engulf all that is and in doing so, capture your own heart. This is self-love, my friend. This is self-love. Precious are the days and ways in which we salute the many by being true to our own heart. Tame the mind and rule the heart in safety and deep comfort. The spinning of the wheel is done from the axis, the pivotal point. The spinning of truth is always from the heart center.

Go forward and be free in all you do.

You are the wind's nemesis, for your breadth is that freedom the wind has, but does not possess. The freedom you have is yours eternally. Open your arms to this life-long freedom, recognized by many as love alone. Recognize your truth and then, let it go, to be the expansion you are. Let the wonder of your open heart ride the waves and settle, ride the waves and settle, knowing it is in the settling our truth shines.

We belong with all in our settled view. Settle to regain your vision and clarity of purpose.

Be the universal wish the world has waited for.

Connections

Welcome to the more of you
The grass so green, the sky so blue
A beautiful heart arrives today
To say; beyond words, what hearts can say

A soul connection ringing true
The spice of life is this true-blue
Acclamations, bells of soul
Pieces present, towards the whole

Blood and tissue, hair and bone
Now ascending to the throne
Overcoming, from before
Setting free and seeing more

There is a script we cannot see
No *play of plays* just *let it be*
Between the acts, no prompts, no sets
And what you see is what you get

Say the love you see you are
Then, keep on speaking and raise the bar
The love you say will never die
So, Hidee-Ho and touch the sky

Relationship

Winter white presents itself in hues of green and gold
The ashes of the truth, within, are never left untold
Between the isles of milk and cheese, the mysteries unfold
The mirror of the mizzenmast is warm, within the hold

I lie with you, you lie with me; the isinglass reveals
A southern wind, so warm and wet, the essence is: to feel
All life and living every swell, divided by the keel
The innocence of constant love; as seen in full appeal

The bell rings out as liberty; a clean, unfurled flag
If this old flag had been a dog, 'twould surely be the wag
If this had been the horse of life, it wouldn't be the nag
Beneath the mould of yesteryears, a glint, a gleam, a crag

All love holds to the breast of breasts and lets the milk flow free
In nourishing, nurturing, kindness-flow; relax and let it be
The King and Queen of kindness bear a Holy Child of glee
This Child, in children everywhere; now, sees Love holds the key

Prayer of Gratitude

By the light of a new moon
Where there are no borders to bind us
Let us pray the prayer of gratitude *now*
Offering up prayer for new beginnings
And blessings for endings
Remembering only
The continuum of love alone
That runs through us all
Like the gentle *breeze* that blows us
Everlasting to everlasting
Let it be

Leftovers

Ruth liked cooking. She was a good cook. Cooking was like chemistry to Ruth. She knew how foods tasted in combination and what spices worked well together to produce desired results. She took pride in her creative kitchen savvy. Combining many recipes into one superb masterpiece was a no-brainer for Ruth.

Early marriage cook-fests brought unexpected kudos from family and friends, and Ruth's culinary confidence steadily grew. She ventured into foreign fare and surprised herself with her successes. "You have the knack!" her husband, Vergne, would say. "This is so good!"

Looking back today on her cooking past, Ruth wondered how she had come to this standoff. Three children and a hurried lifestyle, including full-time work, had led to quick dishes and fussy eaters who turned their noses up at leftovers. This particular evening, the fridge was bursting with partial remnants of the week's meals. How could Ruth re-invent these consumables to avoid waste and provide a family meal everyone would like? She dreamed of a time when she and Vergne would be free to treat themselves to a relaxing meal out.

Zing! A plan formed in Ruth's head and started abuilding.

By the time Vergne arrived home, all of the children were involved in Ruth's plan. Clyde greeted Vergne at the door and informed him that dinner would be served in fifteen minutes. All three children were excited and secretive. Vergne washed up and was escorted to the dining room table by Clyde. Martha Jane presented Vergne with a beautiful handmade menu, complete with collaged food pictures pasted in the margins. Holly waited for what she thought was a respectable amount of time and then rushed in with her pad and pen to take her father's dinner order.

Every fridge leftover was present on the menu, but its name didn't reveal its previous identity.

This cooking game became a fun family tradition for many years in the Brown household and was even rehashed when the retelling of this story sparked the grandchildren's imagination.

Restaurant Night was born!

Mr. Foster

risp white clouds part and joyous bells ring. You own the coveted crown. Gently rest in the everlasting love you are, that is light particulate, everywhere. Let the sun shine to you and through you. Receive and shine. As you shine, you will heal those around you. Let your mettle show. Ride on the waves of completion and deep knowing. You are alive and free to simply be. With deep knowing, access divine love.

Mr. Foster blew the work horn and headed for home. His feet found the pavement and his head found the clouds. The miles between were a forgotten territory—a no-man's land. Keeping quiet, Mr. Foster felt gentle breezes etch a pattern in the already established shore waves. They revealed a freedom, an unexpected break of habit, and eloquence that no words could convey as brilliantly as this erratic flow. Alone, at this moment, Mr. Foster delved into this unexpected uprising and all of its reverie. It made him sing so loud that the birds stopped their pecking at the shore to regard him warily before commencing their forage in washed-up sea kelp.

Set amidst the rivulets of shore wash was an elevated glint of blue crystal. The sun magnified the blue glow as the water parted and the salty brine rushed back to sea. In the softness of his own spacious gaze, Mr. Foster saw the crystal blue as a long line of blue reflected across the wet sand. It was startlingly beautiful and stood out against the beige of the sandy surf.

Like the moon, this blue reflected magic and other-worldliness. It whispered untapped potential and inner madness in one.

Mr. Foster remembered a moonlit night long ago beside the Wambent River with Sarah Brooks. The fiery glinting of her blue eyes haunted him still. Gazing at the blue crystal refraction on the beach, he came unglued. What would ever make me relapse into this nostalgia? he thought. Childhood remembrances are fraught with angst and uncertainty at best. It's time to get back down to earth and head for home and a nice hot cup of tea. Forgetting the brilliant blue of the beach-crystal and the passion of his old remembrance, Mr. Foster willfully gathered his books and satchel and boarded the bus for home.

He was lighter now than this morning. He would not forget the buoyant nature of this summer dream.

The Play of Night and Day

A night and a day were good friends. They agreed on most everything. There was one thing they had a tiny bit of conflict around
and that was: twisting the future into a band of gold. The day felt
that the band of gold should be smooth, plain and solid. Nothing
else would do. The night, however, held to no such design specifica-
tions. The night knew of the endless creating that is, and so the night
held an absolute view of Live and Let Live: "Accentuate the positive,
Eliminate the negative, Latch on to the affirmative and don't mess
with Mr. In-between." An old song, well remembered. The grandeur
of the night's luxurious darkness and mystery flooded the senses of
the day, and the day began to have daydreams that fully coincided
with the dreams of nightly abundance.

Slowly, slowly, the day began to awaken to the altruistic dream-
time of the universal flow and glow. The day began to exude love in
increasing proportions to the gentle occurrences within the is-ness of
life's natural flow. Nourishing thoughts, ideas and endless creations
were born in increasing numbers. The day became clearer and clearer
about the beauty of the night, until one moment, at 12:00 noon, the
day proclaimed an armistice of deep pink poppies that popped up in
all the fields of battle previously known to the day. Old *Victim Men-
talities* and *Burdens to Bear* released into the night's vastness-of-view.
This occurred in such a gentle way that nobody really noticed, except
everyone felt a lot lighter.

People from the West began loving the ancient ways of the East.
People from the East loved the bold new ways of the West. People
from the South united with the true North strong and free, and the
northern spirit coalesced with the southern hospitality, creating soul
food for all. This shifting was all a cosmic coincidence, it seemed,
and yet many people had seen it coming and heralded its arrival
with trumpets of their own making from flowers of their choice.

Step by step we create the dream. Step by step we dismantle the dream and let it go to recreate a new dream, with all. The wall of the past is a fallen shrine that, in its falling, unblocked the door to peace within and without. This opening is a peace portal that has created itself through us all as a heart's desire to be free and secure in our place of natural being with all life.

The incendiaries are quiet now. The insecure places from whence the bombs were dropped are fading quickly and quietly and a peace-filled portal can be seen clearly in the lifting mists of time. It is such a large portal; it has no borders or boundaries. It is timeless and whole in its approach to silent-being.

The mouse was the first to run through the portal. He is the explorer in us all. He could hardly wait to explore this new reality presenting. He crossed the portal threshold and stood up on his hind legs to take in life with all of his senses. Just then, an eagle lifted him up to a higher view and suddenly, he remembered who he was! He was both the dream and the dreamer. He was both this creation and its creator. The mouse relaxed into his own reality. He held no fear or apprehension. It didn't make sense that he would. How could he fear that which he had created with all? He knew he could not get life wrong. He saw clearly that life would, happily, never get done. He felt the endless creation of his life, and it was all a wondrous adventure of endless expansion. He accepted his wholeness and the wholeness of all that is.

Web-Central

Sometimes spider would accept the day as it is. He would wake up on the center of the web. He would be well aware of vibes in every direction. He would know who he was, and this would greatly ease his mind. His shoes would be off and his feet would feel the grounding of the web upon which he lived. Here, in the Web-Central, spider had a handle on every golden strand of his connection to all life. He could feel the flow and glow. He could sense the easy depth of his connection.

One day, a petunia by the name of Sally came by unexpectedly. She rose from her flowerbed and felt spider at work among her petals. Feeling included in the connections of others made Sally very curious. She decided to inquire about spider's glue and the hue of his web upon her open flower.

"Spider," she began, "do you know who I am?"

"Of course I do!" replied spider. "You are the beauty of life presenting at the edge of my understanding. I have always known you!"

"Thank you," said Sally. "I feel your web upon my petals and it intrigues me to know our deeper connection."

"You are the red in my green," said the spider. "You are the turquoise in my orange. We go together in such a complementary way. I could not imagine my life without your sweet face to connect to. You are a part of the glue that holds my web in place."

Sally felt what spider talked about through her floral expression. It tickled her deeply to hear about her natural expression in this unique way. It seemed so preposterous, and yet it felt just right and she loved the feeling within her.

Spider spun a tale for Sally that day. It was a tale of magical spinning. It was a yarn, to be sure, but more than that, it was a continuous thread to Sally's heart that she understood instantly, even before one word was spoken. It was the heart-understanding of a larger, all inclusive, story that never, ever ends but keeps on telling itself. It was a story of inner truth that only truth can tell, understand, interpret and appreciate—all at the same time!

Sally stood very still as she took this story in through all of her senses. She knew this story so deeply. It ran through the height, breadth and depth of her. As she listened to this soft story, that was so wise it could tell itself, she began to trust herself as a perfect part of this endless yarn. She recognized her colour and shine. She knew her form and her ever-flowing, formless design as a part of this story that she recognized as essentially herself.

Spider kept on spinning and spinning, as he always did. Sally kept on connecting and reconnecting to this web that touched her so very deeply, yet she could not say why. In the Now, she did not care or worry about why.

"It just is," she said. "I know this so certainly within the flow I am."

"Make a wish," said the spider. "When you make a wish connected to the web, it always comes true. Did you know that?"

"No," said Sally, "but I can feel the truth of your words flow through me, and your words are alive with vibration because you are so connected to the web."

"It is my way," said the spider. "It has always been my way. Thank you for the wonderful connection, Sally. I feel the flow of your loveliness through my feet, and it grounds me to the truth of my foundation, supporting me. I feel at home in this secure setting that you, too, are so at home in. I know I belong here with you."

"There will be other days and other natural ways, to be sure," said spider, "but I will always remember your truthful connection and your genuine curiosity from within about our connection. Maybe we will meet again and maybe not. I will treasure this time we have shared connected to the web that I have spun to support myself, which is connected to all other life. As I explore all of my connections with curiosity, I will learn about my interconnection with all of life and I will know myself as the endless life story I am, for no part of life does not touch me. I am blessed by every strand of all connection.

"When I beat the drum of my own belonging on the web I weave, I know the co-creator I am with all of life. I know this in my heart-mind, for universal knowing is within my heart center and from this point of interconnection, all of my threads are spun through all of eternity, and so Web-Central is a joyful emotion I feel, from within."

Guided by the light of love

essons received are voiced through love and connection. Accept the truth of your spiritual existence in the All. Delude yourself no further in separate thinking. We are all connected and whole. Play your part in healing yourself and thereby healing others. Accept this role of healer and intuitive. Access your gifts through inner opening.

Breathe in and breathe out and let go of all blocks. Begin to see how this operates in your life. Dwell on the moment and live in the light of existence here and now. Flow in the light of your own inner-shining. Act on your inner guidance and your inner wisdom. Brightness beckons you forward. Heed the light that leads you to action and accomplishment. Push away from the safety of the shore and float in the sea of life. Learn and experience as you float in life's midst.

Steer your own vessel and allow the universal love to float with you and around you. This love will support and nurture you and will guide you to a safe harbour in times of need and darkness. The beauty of the darkness is a lesson learned and a vibration raised.

Seek the truth you require and ask the questions you must ask. See your place among souls and also see your unique lesson. Rise to the task appearing before you and know your own true expression.

Flow with your vibration and create the song that expresses your soul's longing. Connect as you are drawn to do so. Go where you love to go. Explore where you love to explore. Live your life in the light.

Live now.

Examine every pebble of your existence and soar to the full heights availed to you. Spend time in nature to clear and restore your energies. Lend your energy to your heart's desire. Open your heart to see the love present in every situation.

Follow this loving thread to the marrow of your life's work. Clear your heart of trial and a heavy weight. Rise above everyday concerns and take flight into the depths of spiritual life and coexistence with other levels and layers of life. Blend and flow with love and peace.

Transcend time and space and leave all worry behind. Access the All as you step forward to see the truth of life.

The heart does not judge or condemn. The heart loves wholly and completely.

Guidance—Fines Wintworth

Is there a story to relay to all, to delight the child's heart into understanding to what absolute depth it is forever loved?

Fines Wintworth was an athlete. His prowess in the field of athletics was world renowned. He walked like he thought an athlete should walk. He talked like he thought an athlete should talk. He brought home ribbon after ribbon after endless ribbon for winning in one category of athletics after another. He tried every venue and no venue tried him. Fines liked being a household name. It satisfied him deeply.

Then one day, Fines fell seriously ill. He did not know what, exactly, was wrong with him, but he did not feel good at all. He cancelled all of his athletic engagements and took to his bed to try to heal his discomfort from within. He sat, bent over, knelt down, slumped in a chair and finally crawled into his bed and tried to find a comfortable position to ease his discomfort from within. His mother called to see how Fines was making out.

He said, "Fine." He was used to saying fine. It was easier than telling the truth. The truth felt complicated and required explanations and the intimacy of sharing, which Fines felt so awkward about. He steered clear of honesty and told others what he thought they wanted to hear: "I'm fine."

When Fines took to his bed, nobody even noticed, because he had never shared his deep concern about his discomfort with anyone, so everyone who might have shown care and concern didn't even phone or check up on Fines. They just assumed he was fine, like his name.

Fines grew sicker and sicker and finally, he died of causes unknown. As Fines departed this earthly focus, he saw many colours and he traveled, quickly, back to his Source.

From pure Source energy, Fines could see the events of his past life clearly, and he realized the distance he had maintained between himself and others in his heart. He saw that he was a hero in his own mind, and although others appreciated his physical prowess, they felt distant and alienated from him because he did not know how to share his heart. He did not know how to maintain a natural heart connection with all.

A gypsy, on the road to *Consider This*, stopped in to see Fines in his new focus. He had been good to her on many occasions. He did not even realize that he had been good to her until she explained it to him.

"You showed me over and over and over how to trust my physical expression in the world. I thank you for your natural gift. It is beautiful and unique."

"I see I have not remained closely connected to others," Fines said, looking at his life story.

The gypsy replied, "There are many, many levels to a story if you look under the window dressing of its display. The outer layer of your expression is just a mask. It is how you would like others to see you. It is not who you are. I see your light. You have shown me my strength to proceed in a physical focus. I cannot thank you enough for this.

"When I doubted my reason for being here and now, you would show up and demonstrate persistence and achievement, and I would see self-trust in your eyes and in your physical reflection. Thank you for following your heart's desire. You have taught others to do the same. Your truthful expression speaks louder than words. It tells a story of endurance and focus, and it tells a story of love-alone, no matter what you are thinking. In every moment, when you make a deep decision to express honestly and openly, you cannot imagine the beauty of your heart's sharing.

"Love will use you as an anchor of understanding when you do from your heart. Be still and listen. The voice that directed your

heart to athletic prowess will direct your heart to self-healing. You
need only to be still and listen to your inner voice calling:

"Come this way, child, come this way. True love is this way."

Freedom

Write from this pool of soft flow, this well of sparkling, effervescent, scintillating view, where nights are days and wells of ink leak magic onto a page with the readiness of sprites and leprechauns. Eels dance their oily slippers over muskeg mixed with the salty brine of eons past.

Spread me wider than wide to taste from every cup. Burrow through sinew, through muscle, through trust to a page so ready to receive, its vibrancy rises to touch the pen of all thought, soaking from it all of the choked words of yesterday.

Make ready the pen of this day of blissful flow. Let it ride the waves of every understanding and every disappointment and never flail on the beach of discontentment, feeling alone and voiceless. No, this pen has many stories to tell: of terror, of vibrancies, of caution, of truth, of litmus excursions into emotional waters and mountains climbed. Arrest this pen for no crimes. She is free to be. In preparation for this journey, she has rested long and now, steeped in her own juices, flows as she goes.

"Pen, meet freedom—freedom, pen."

"Oh, freedom, I have heard so much about you. My heart rises to meet your wings and my ink quivers within at our possibilities. Send your truth to the hand that guides me, freedom. My bags are packed and the door is open. Within my flow, we can travel, car-less, beyond time and escape the earth-bonds to magical thought and inner delight."

Walk down an old street in a different direction and find your flow. See the freshness of new glints and captivating angles. The wide-open pastures of the mind can be brought to every nuance of living. The imaginings of perfection that we overlay on newly discovered territory could also transform the seemingly mundane of the known.

It is the view that writes the song, picks the notes and sets the tone of all existence, no other.

Storyline

Tomorrow is the story of many stories," the spider said to his friend the beetle. "They are tied together with a storyline.

"A storyline is a familiar chord that runs through the whole fabric of a story and sets a theme for the over and under view while maintaining a view of what is, now.

"Do you understand?"

The beetle rearranged his under-wings and flexed his long antennae uncertainly, pondering the "storyline" proposition. "Is this a question or a known fact?" he asked.

"It is a heart-understanding," the spider said. "You must feel it to discern its depth of proposal."

"Oh!" said the beetle. "I see."

The spider, who was used to telling stories, continued along the same thread. "In the findings found in any story there is some repression, some embellishment and a tiny bit of freedom or truth that is sandwiched in the middle to hold the whole thing together as a cohesive whole. There is a beginning, a main part and a wrapping-up or ending to tie it off as a pattern of its own design."

The beetle was intrigued now. He loved stories.

He had never stopped to delve into stories or discuss them in depth like this, but he felt joyful at the very idea of a story being told. He could get right into it and feel he was living it himself. In this way, he could do things he would never consider in any other circumstance.

He could dive fearlessly in at the deep end, knowing a story would not drown him or overwhelm his senses. He could easily flow along with it, and so he could certainly see how this pull towards stories might be what spider called a "storyline." It was a line that pulled you to stay and experience the next part and the next and the next.

Yes, he thought. This must be a storyline.

How interesting. He had known this all along, but had never stopped to sort it out for himself!

Spider continued, "The strain in a story can sometimes wear on a storyline and cause it to unravel altogether, you know. I told a " story to a group of ants last week and as the excitement built and the ants responded by getting tense, someone sneezed with such force, the storyline just broke right off and the ants laughed and laughed at this unexpected turn in the storyline. That was funnier than the story itself."

"A new story was spawned from the old storyline and it had a life of its own."

Beetle could picture this happening. He knew of several times in his short life where this had occurred and he had wondered why he could not hold the attention of a group of listeners. He now saw how this could be. The naturalness of it put his mind and heart at ease. Storytelling was just a gentle occurrence and nothing more.

Spider was feeling confident now. She was hanging by one leg and drawing circles with the other seven. The halo on her head was visible.

"A long time ago in the vastness of Now, a valiant prince rode a horse with a bridle of purest gold," she began. "This bridle was not for pulling or pushing the horse, for this horse knew its way to go at every turn. This bridle was significant because it showed the prince's station in life. It showed that this prince knew well of the golden light that creates all. The prince had not always felt he knew this. It had been a long, hard-won battle that he had fought within himself to come to this place of self-recognition. He could see his true essence and know his face with certainty in a crowd. There were dragons to be slain and witches to overcome. There were panthers to face in the night and many uncertainties to reconsider.

"The half-truths were the second part of the prince's journey. Some of them were sticky. Others were sullen and illusive. He sifted through them all and became wiser in the ways of men.

"The third part of the prince's journey involved a chain that he wore around his ankle. It tied him to the past and to the future. Only through trial and error did he see the delusive nature of this chain. He saw that he had always been free. He just needed to see it in a new way. He needed to see it from his heart.

"He needed to be heart-smart to say, 'I am free. I am me. I can see. All is well.'

"As these words were spoken from his heart, the golden light came in of its own accord and a golden bridle was placed upon his horse. The prince was a catalyst for peace wherever he went. It was his bent.

"He was never bent out of shape again."

Universal Connection

As the night fell upon the land of Now, an old song began to play itself very, very softly. It was both a song of joy and a song of gentle fruition. There was an interlude of longing to this song that cascaded from the mountaintops down to the valley floor. It was a song of fruit ripening and of falling off the tree of life. It was a song of harmonious co-creation. It was a song of gently abiding with all things. It was a song of peace. It was a song of natural contrast. It was a song of laughter's easy way. It was a song of children at play. It was a song of the grandmother's grace. It was a song of the grandfather's knowledge. It contained all that ever was in a whisper. It contained nothing at all and even less than that.

As this song began to be heard by all, its gentleness crept quietly into all hearts. Soon, heart-lights began to come on in the valley and curious inquisitions of the heart-strings came into play. Souls were tickled as if by a feather, and freedom was felt as a cool, soft mist rolling across the land.

The first to feel this song were the children. This song gave them a sense of quietude and belonging. Some of the children were very tired from waiting for this song's arrival. They had felt this song so deeply, they could sense its vibration in their teeth and jaws.

On the night this song was born again into the world, two spirits of light made a pact to assist it on its journey into time. They remembered the roots of this song so deeply in their souls that even a slight inference would bring tears to their eyes.

Not far from where you live, there is an open-hearted meadow where these two spirits connect. It is not a meadow of physical focus. It is a meadow of the heart-mind and leaving all thought behind, where these two spirits of light connect and play this song together for everyone to hear and appreciate.

There is another connection these two light spirits have, and that is one of trust in the song that so touches their souls. When the universal song plays itself through these two, they have no doubt about their being. They connect with others through this oneness-song.

There are no words to this song—no right and no wrong.
There is no melodious chirping like a bird song.
There is no water whooshing, like a whale song.
There is no call-of-the-wild like a loon song.
There is no whip, whip, whip of the *Whip-poor-will*.
There is only the soft undertoning of the light of love, and a connecting bond of everlasting love is recognized and loosely held as it is.

Creative weavings

On top of a ridge, by a laughing waterfall, resided a witch. She was a witch of humour and good taste. She was a wise one of millennia gone by. She was an omen of the long-sought-after peace that no one could seem to find. This witch was a truant, for she was hard to find at the best of times and impossible to find when things ran amok. Malley was the witch's name. She had been O'Malley, but she dropped the O; it seemed superfluous, and she was a straight-talker. Malley was a purposeful dreamer of dreams. She never lacked for dreams or the exuberance to talk about them. The winds of change would blow and blow and Malley would remain in her dreams and spin a web of finest gold to share with all.

One such dreamy evening, Malley was just winding up one dream and starting another when a spider came by to see what she was spinning. She seemed to be drawing folks in with her dreams, and the spider wanted a closer look at her connecting thread and the patterns she spun.

At first, all the spider could see was a long, anchored thread that went right down and right up from where Malley stood. Then, as the spider's eyes adjusted to the subtle lighting of dusk, he could see the interweaving of the stories, where Malley had dipped into the Fruit-of-the-Loom to bring forth Lavender essence or Hollyhocks so tall, you had to look up to see their blooms. Everything was here as fodder for Malley's weavings.

Spider saw the whole of it and smiled the smile of a storyteller.

"I see!" spider said, thoughtfully holding the one long whisker on his chin.

Morning brought a touch of magic to the ridge-walker's village. Spider had been up all night. He had spun and spun and now slept by the side of his latest weaving. The patterns were beautiful and endless. The filament was strong and connected. The vibration was solid and not to be missed. The morning dew had settled along the rows of the web, and within each dew drop could be seen a spot of gold reflected into the eyes of onlookers.

No one had seen such a sight before. It was brilliant and yet so natural. It made perfect sense. It was warm and calming, but electrifying and exciting too. The canvas upon which spider had displayed his web was a beautiful old Eucalyptus branch, and the smell of Eucalyptus played on the wind and relaxed the ridge folk.

The honing of spider's skills had begun. He could feel it in his bones. The natural expression of his being was on display. He looked and looked at his creations. He never seemed to get tired of creating. He loved it. He could spin all night with pure delight, then rest for awhile and begin again. He went back to the witch to say thank you for her teachings. The witch received his thanks with gratitude. She was so happy that spider had found the way to his natural expression.

She came to see spider's webs. She marveled at their natural flow and the endless connection within them all.

She was so inspired, she felt she must weave another dream.

Follow Your Heart

On most Saturday mornings, Elise Williams rose and went about her morning tasks of leveling the laundry pile and tackling the mountain of dishes in the sink. She found these tasks tiring at times, but usually this routine embodied a letting-go process that was hard to explain, even to herself. There was the sorting of the laundry; the gathering of it from every far-flung corner of the house—the towels, washcloths, mats and sweaty biking clothes drying on the basement rack. Then there was the locating of the dishes from up and downstairs and getting the dishwasher filled and started before tackling the pots and pans. Garbage collection was next; sorting the recycling into bins and all else into the outside trash.

Once this Saturday process had begun and felt in hand, Elise would begin to consider other things she might want to do with her day. Her mind would now be centered and focused and *ready for action*, as she called it.

Thus it was that one Saturday morning, Elise Williams decided to step out of her usual pattern. She stood up beside her bed, stretched her arms above her head and yawned widely. She decided to do exactly what her heart desired first.

The first thing that came to mind was her dog, Stew. He came bounding into the bedroom full of life and licked Elise's hand, rubbing his velvety ears against her legs and singing in high, excited yips.

"Wanna go for a walk?" Elise asked eagerly. "C'mon, buddy, c'mon, let's go outside and greet the day together, okay?" Stew knew the drill of that tone of voice, and he ran straight to the red jacket with the dog leash coiled in the pocket. He jumped up and down joyfully with straight front legs. Elise threw on her sweatpants and oversized T-shirt, donned the now slobbery red jacket, and off these two strolled in perfect sync.

Elise took a right turn at the end of the alley leading into the meadow, and she let Stew lead the way. Stew, off the leash, kept looking back to make sure Elise was still well in view, still connected with him. They had sunk into this comfortable understanding of togetherness by getting to know each other's patterns and accommodating each other with ease and constant appreciation, since Stew was a pup. Time went out the window when Elise and Stew were together. Life became a dream of their creating. They explored every valley and knoll, root and stump, dandelion and moth, delighting in each other's presence with life presenting.

The odd thing about this combination of woman and dog was that neither categorized themselves in their togetherness. Woman was dog and dog was woman and who cared anyway? The most beautiful moments became a thread of such strong connection, such a focused bond, that lightness was their understanding. There was no unevenness in their relating. They rejoiced in each other's presence and didn't notice who saw. It was an unselfconscious, unspoken agreement to honour the beauty of their love, no matter the subtle differences in their unique expression in the world. It was a deep decision for love without masks or conditions. It was a soul decision to be each other's biggest fan.

Class-consciousness

Class-consciousness is keeping us all apart. It is an enigma of a fundamental warlord system set up so very long ago, and it serves no part of us well. It is an absolute misunderstanding that we hold in our daily view of living and yet continues to remain completely untrue and unfitting for us all. We are beings of the light. We are simply and completely source energy—focused into a physical reality here on earth. This physical focus is only a tiny part of the source energy we are. The larger non-physical part of us is always with us when we tune in and turn on to it. There are no exceptions to this. We are lesser or better than none. We are the stuff that dreams are made of and together, in every single moment, we are co-creating a beautiful dream. It is a dream of unveiling all of the energy centers of the universe to reveal the gentle strength of love-alone at the core of all that naturally is.

The natives of our land were a gentle people who were so cognizant of this gentle truth living within us all. They understood the honouring of the ancestors, animals, trees, flowers and all life. They gave thanks for all that was supplied and they lived off the land and with all things—simply and creatively, knowing that all are a part of this journeying we do together and all contribute to it in their own way. The natives honoured the unique expression of life as it is. They were as children in their simple expression of living.

The debt that we have incurred is huge now. We are in the hole. This hole is so very near to our faces, we find it hard to look through to the next stage of our evolution, because we are looking outside of ourselves and a sense of lack is what we are seeing with our eyes.

When we look more deeply, we are still. In our stillness, we focus within to see what everyone is looking at. It is the love that is everywhere. It is the eternal balance of the void in our life that we are staring at so intently. Together, these two aspects of our life essence create a natural balance. You will show up in someone else's life to create a contrast for them to see their light more clearly, and the light of love shows up in your life as you realize that what you are experiencing is not what you are wanting. You do not feel good.

Your friend within is your eternal feeling capability. You are a sentient being. It is your ultimate capability to feel, very deeply and certainly, the energy all around you. This subtle and not-so-subtle sense is telling you all the time if you are flowing with the stream of life or struggling upstream by doing, doing, doing and not being the sentient, all-knowing being you are. The contrast shows up to the extent that you are vibrating away from what your inner desire is. If your desire is to hear 105.9 FM and you are tuned into 860 AM, you are not getting what you are wanting and you know it by the way you feel about it. This contrast or not feeling good is your indication to change direction, give up the struggle and flow with the river of life to naturally move towards what you are wanting.

Allow the natural flow of your life to take you exactly where you need to go. You will see, through your own unique experiencing of your living, that ease and grace will just show up at your doorstep if you take your oars out of the water and let love turn your boat around as you stop paddling upstream. You need to allow yourself to experience this to believe it. Once you understand your process, you will trust it more and more.

No one can control your thoughts unless you allow them to. You are free to love yourself and follow your heart in your thoughts in your own self-created dream.

You are an energy being first and foremost, focused into a physical reality, and there is an endless supply of love and light all around you. If you are still and look within, you will see yourself clearly, with love. You will know with deep certainty that you are. A vibration of absolute love will be your constant companion.

Consider the source of the thoughts you are buying into most strongly now. Look beneath this and feel who you are. You are free. You are an endless supply of source energy that never dies except to the old view. Your focus into the physical is the only cross you bear. The reason going within and finding peace sounds trite to so many people is because it is often heard of and talked about, but few people actually make a decision to love themselves in this way. Once you have this deep experience, you will not be able to deny yourself any longer. You will feel the beauty of the peace at your core. It is the quiet strength that is always there for you to tap into. You will begin to understand who you are from your spacious heart. You will begin to love yourself the way no one else can.

Life Force

Life is an ever-changing, uninterruptible force in the universe. It moves and adjusts in perfect order to accommodate all heart's desire, as it is energetically sent out. The frequency that we are sending out with our thoughts attracts everything of that same vibration to us, and this is how we create our lives alone and together at once.

In the time/space past, the laws of the church presided over our living in so strong a fashion that we still carry some old consciousness of carefully judging ourselves, and what we perceive as others, for sins or transgressions against man-created laws. This old hold that pervaded our space is letting go and moving into the love that is, allowing us freedom as far as the inner eye can see and that is a long way, baby—forever more!

Old anchors of *unworthiness, unsafe* and shame-based *fear* reside in the pit of our stomach. We have gut reactions when a new thought is presented, and we do not know why. We have a stomach ache in anticipation of a new event or of meeting a new person, and we wonder what this is. It is an old consciousness rising up to be set free. Bless it all! Thoughts cannot harm you unless you repress your true feelings, rising up, about them. Allow your feelings space to express how this self-repression of true emotion feels. Then feel the power of this honest expression. The truth of honest expression will, as the saying goes, set you free. You have only to try it to see.

All is well in the universe any way it *is*. Life is eternally shifting and balancing and figuring out the best way to go, because it is one absolute consciousness of all and we are all driving this bus, together.

In understanding the above, then it makes perfect sense aboard this absolute bus:

That we would all decide, together, that the majority desires will
cause the turns and ups and downs in direction;

That we would all see scenery that all are presenting in their unique
   focus of life from this bus;
That the wheel of this bus might be hard to turn at times and easier
   at others;
That there would be some discrepancies, within the consciousness in
   this bus, according to placement and view from that placement;
That some cannot see the highway from where they are seated upon
   this bus and when others leave, these may move to a window seat;
That some have a split-focus from watching those who are projecting,
   coughing, sneezing or acting out on this bus;
That some have their eyes closed and are sleeping;
That some are unaware of the natural laws of this bus and move, by
   default, with currently held beliefs;
That some are leaping off this bus because it is too loud, quiet,
   uncontrolled, in their face, abundant, unexpected or simple;
That all passengers know deeply that they belong together no matter
   what present life looks like;
That the interior lights are coming on as night falls upon this bus;
That we, the driver, are becoming more responsible for the loving
   energy-source of this bus;
That we are all becoming adjusted to each other out of necessity and,
   in our adjustment, we are beginning to see our family connec-
   tions past our disconnects;
That a humorous hum is being heard from the children on this bus;
That all are looking towards this new tune in wonder at its harmony
   and lightness;
That as we gaze, slack-jawed, at the beauty presenting on this bus; we
   are seeing our own beautiful love-ability, together;
That the children have always been the teachers on this bus;
That this has been a long ride to self-unity;
That unity with all in this bus is on the horizon and we need to look
   up to see it;
That everlasting source-energy is everywhere for this bus ride;

That the hum of the children is becoming a song;
That those on this bus ride know to sing along;
That the flow of this bus ride is starting to move;
That everyone present moves into the groove;
That silence and prayer are the light that we keep;
That living this love, with all others, is cheap;
That as we progress, we see light on the wall;
That in this reflection, we start to stand tall;
That in this type of standing, we're moving with Grace;
That the wall we are passing is just a fear-face;
That the bus of our business is starting to grind;
That the cogs of its wheels now mesh with heart-mind;
That in minding the store of all our treasures within;
That we're now seeing wealth in the state we are in.

The Traffic Cop

Once upon a time, in the Lane of Change and Misdirection, there lived a traffic cop who was sick and tired of the endless chaos of the traffic he conducted. When he was young, the traffic didn't seem to bother him. In aging, he felt incapable of maintaining this level of anxiety and uncertainty. He thought to himself, Rest for awhile and you will feel revived to continue in the same vein. He rested, but it did not work. He was not at all enthused to return to the fray of his daily, hectic existence.

At the end of a particularly frenetic day, he loosened his tie and sat down in the gentle breeze under a nearby sycamore tree. He felt deeply grateful for the tree and its protection, and he didn't know why. He wondered about this. He gazed at the heat rising from the pavement and the patterns it presented. He found this fascinating. As soon as he thought about the pattern and looked more closely, it was gone. He rubbed his eyes and felt the cooling breeze. He smelled the scent of the sycamore and it was heavenly to him. He drew in a deep breath and released it. He fell back into his softly gazing state of observing the visible heat waves rising from the asphalt. I wonder, he thought, if I maintain this gaze, can I see other patterns I haven't seen before? He shifted his gaze slowly to the fountain in the middle of the traffic circle. Soon he could see rainbow patterns in the mist of the fountain's spray. What else am I not seeing, he thought? I like this soft, gazing view.

All night, the cop kept waking and remembering the feeling of seeing these subtle, almost hidden, patterns.

By special dispensation, the cop asked to be moved to a quieter street. He knew he needed to slow down and take stock of his own patterns to see the beauty of life again. Night found the cop happy with his heart-decision and eager to begin his work in a new way. He arrived on the job early to observe the traffic flow and get a bird's-eye view of details his job might entail. This street was called Ambrosia. It didn't have a fountain, but it dripped with flower baskets filled with hyacinth and grapevine. The smell filled his heart. In the distance, birdsong caught his ears, and he knew that if the birds liked it here, he would too. It was almost 9:00 AM, and his shift began. He wanted to try his soft gazing and see if it could apply to other things as well. Sure enough, it did. If he gazed softly at the rushing pedestrians, they looked like a multi-coloured flow of stop and go. If he gazed softly at the rush-hour traffic, it became a blur of colour and lights. It was coffee time and lunch time before the cop knew it, and then, he was walking along Glory Street on his way home.

What a change, he thought. I couldn't have imagined this relaxing shift in view. It was something I needed to experience first, and then I could experiment with it to find a new way to see my life. A bird sang, as if to confirm the cop's new understanding. Just then, the cop looked up. A cloud pattern displayed a porpoise leaping high across the sky.

Wow! The cop thought. This has been a day with a golden trim. In this new, more relaxed focus, I can actually feel the deeper life pattern I am seeing.

Life

"Carol did not write of heroes or heroines; she wrote of ordinary, yet extraordinary, people—like we all are. She saw the hugely special in each person she met and in everything she saw and experienced. Her family said she had many more books in her to write. She lived each moment of her later life writing, until she passed."

Carol Shields, a beloved Canadian novelist, died in July 2003, following a long struggle with breast cancer. I heard about her death on the CBC Radio, while riding home from Vancouver. Listening to an inspired view of her life (above) by her publisher and a clip from one of her books touched my heart and the flame inside of me to write.

Unique and whole, we come into our lessons equipped with tools. Blessed beyond our understanding, we struggle with our wounded hearts until we see an inner light to warm and nurture ourselves by—through all we encounter. The knowing of this deep *eternal truth* changes the coin of barter in our living. We need never sell our souls to live again. Our masks lie, strewn behind us with relief and a relaxed breath. Finally, we see the deep possibilities to nurture others and ourselves. Uncertain, we take our first steps along our path of light to learn and grow in spiritual stature. Trusting our source, we flow and grow.

Bright beacons show us glimpses of another reality. We feel the energy that flows in and around us. It confirms our humanity. We are free to fly, and in our flying, expand. We are brighter than ever we thought possible. Our certainty of purpose is in our cells. It strengthens from our marrow and as we sense the illusion of control we thought so real, our sense of creativity and fun arrives.

Our happy heart opens wide to our inner child and the

innocence in all. We are one, together, pulsing in a universal dance of light and dark, colour and illumination. The gossamer of the universe touches every part of our life-flow.

Being still, we reach out and connect to something we know is truth. A flow begins and heals us as it dismisses the clouds of fault and delusion obscuring our inner sun. Enveloped in our shining, we see where we have been and forgive all. We see more fully the non-productive nature of judgment and surrender to an ease of living afloat this sea of energy. Taming our minds, to see that only love empowers us. A soft, non-reactive certainty arises. An inner-leopard of light becomes the leader we follow. Pain and uncertainty become our lessons.

Searching and reflection lead to some understanding of our infinite, timeless self. Guides and angels assist where a sincere reaching-out occurs. All we require is a spacious heart. Our unique capabilities are limitless. We bestow this natural blessing upon our soul-self. Seeing this is the key to fuller sight.

Here, in silence, we may strive to know ourselves deeply in all of our aspects—not just physical or mental, but eternal and free to be. We fly through the night of our uncertainty and fear into the light of our brilliance. We are never separated from this ever-present life-flow except by our own choosing to ignore an integral part of our self. As we stand our narrow, worldly-view aside and search our inner desires and sources of delight, we surface to breathe more fully.

Life animates our body and lights our eyes.

Montis Moudri Remembers

Friday morning at 9:00 AM, Montis Moudri finished what he was working on and headed out on his morning walk. It was a more of a stroll, actually. Montis loved to walk through the bits and bites of forest near his home. He became blissful at the very remembrance of feeling uplifted by the forest energy and grounded by the earth under his two flat feet.

On this particular morning, Montis was more than ready for his daily walk. He had ungrounded himself by putting his thinking cap on so tightly that it was quite attached to his head and his head to it. Montis longed to fully feel the natural grounded-flow of the forest in his whole being. He left his desk, his facts and figures and his as yet unresolved decisions on his desktop. He put on his most comfortable walking shoes and socks. He put on his old, sweaty hiking shirt and out the door he went.

Montis walked through the park at the very end of the street. He said hello to his favourite cedar tree, there beside the beaten path. As he continued towards the forest road that he walked daily, he remained fully present for himself, within. He tuned into his deep core-energetic easily and he felt the peace and calm of his higher self inside. There was a long rocky section along the way to the forest road, and Montis particularly loved this area. It reminded him of the bumps and hard knocks in his life that he had seen as obstacles at one time because he carried a charged perspective about them in his mind. Now Montis danced through these perceived obstacles with ease and a willing middle focus of understanding that nothing at all is intrinsically good or bad.

Montis made a decision to focus in a non-polarized way. He found that every thought was present to tune into. Through practice, he learned to tune into the thoughts that made him happy. It wasn't that Montis had an aversion to perceived badness or dark thoughts. It was that he understood the positive power of his own deep intention to be his true soul-self without feeling hemmed in, imprisoned or guarded in his view of thoughts. Montis had felt and dealt with all of his energetic phases and he understood clearly the depth of hell he could easily take himself into with a negative view feeding his fear.

Montis passed the length of the rocky patch on the trail without hypervigilance. He hit the forest road and felt the cool of the shade trees along both sides of him. He took a deep, cleansing breath and smiled at his good fortune to have taken this time to connect more deeply with his senses.

All of the stuck-thoughts flew off the back of Montis' head and into the fresh forest airwaves. He felt refreshed and renewed. He felt lighter and certainly brighter than his recent computer configurations. He began to whistle and then, to sing out loud—softly at first and then loudly as he strode forward joyfully. His feet made the rhythm section for a new song creating itself through him. Montis often received vivid understandings of old songs that his father had sung in the early mornings of his youth but now the lyrics would be different:

"Action makes the heart beat faster. Forests soothe the heated brow. Moving in the early morning lets me find a song somehow."

He marched to his own grounded beat, accepting the wind rearranging his hair. He accepted sun and shadow's warm and cold. He accepted a new frame of reference. Montis flowed himself into feeling well and uncomplicated, like any flower or piece of grass. Montis allowed his whole self to naturally glow.

Montis stopped beside a flowing stream to tell it about the loss of his beloved cat. The brook listened quietly. Montis took off his shoes to plunge his hot feet into the cool, rippling stream. After a long, cool foot-bath, Montis felt less agitated. He felt in tune with the natural affairs of nature. He quit fighting himself. He saw nature's way all around him, peacefully allowing its own unique subtle expression without muss or fuss. Montis knew he could do the same with his inner focus. He didn't have to hold onto his fear of his cat's passing. He let go and knew in his heart that he and his cat would never be apart. They were natural friends. They were so easy with each other. Montis would not forget this deep feeling. He would hold his cat's memory safely in his heart.

Montis remembered the time that a friend of his came by to say hello and ask how life was going. This friend truly knew the depth of Montis' connection to him. Even though Montis had been apart from this friend for ten years, it was timeless. They just picked up the thread of their natural relationship. They sat in the garden under the broad maple tree and reminded each other about how damn good it feels to gut-laugh; to be complete fools again and get in touch even more deeply. This was a surprise to Montis. He had thought that he and his friend were already close. Now he could see that there was no end to the depth of connection possible. He was willing to go soul-deep with his old friend. They talked about the pain of Montis's cat's death and they actually called it death without pussyfooting around. Together, they could face it squarely and talk about the grief of endings and the beauty of remembering natural animal connection.

Montis had heard as a child, "Sad as it may seem, all things die that are born or have a mother." He thought this must include all life. Life's cycles are natural and inevitable. He knew this, yet he had felt surprised over and over as the inevitable occurrence of death took place and he was left in its wake to pick up his own piece of understanding and continue in a new way each day to accept and integrate the change.

Montis thought about change a lot on his walks. He thought about all life evolving in its own way. He thought about his own natural, individuated expression and how he used to react so much and now mostly responded to change beyond any thoughts at all. He felt grateful for the grace of being evolutionary consciousness and what learning this had brought to his life. He felt grateful for being deeply sentient. He knew that deep feelings had taught him which way to move in the world to feel better inside. He knew that feeling was a clear indicator of yes or no. Montis adjusted his ball cap and walked more upright with the wind. He let the wind assist him on the home stretch.

More than the unexpected grace that presents to arrange life into something more elaborate, Montis knew the simplicity of the deeper wind blowing his life around. He opened up the inner door of his heart. He invited this gentle wind in. He knew the purpose of this wind was to blow him back to himself, against nothing and with all. The blustery wind settled. The mettle of the life in Montis Moudri felt strong, yet flexible, to change and naturally rearrange itself to suit the soul-essence within him, inherently remembering everything. Montis saw, from his perspective of wholeness, that in his unlimited view he was indeed a co-creation, creating endlessly with all life.

In the unlimited sway of the endless wind, Montis felt freer to just be still than he had ever felt before. He felt gratitude ripple through his body. He blessed himself as the universal flow he is with all life-flow. He knew that he could do anything he set his mind and heart to. The blue of his true-blue expression felt comfortable to express naturally, as his heart saw fit. His pit of despair had taught him so much about where he wanted to go to flow with all that is love. All that is now, unfolding, had found Montis, and he could not wipe the grin of soul-satisfaction off his face.

"Welcome to the human race!" he said. "The best of both worlds is right here, right now, as I am!"

The Blind Man Sees

T omorrow and tomorrow and tomorrow," said the blind man to
himself. "Tomorrow is all I hear, right here and now in this open
space of all spaciousness that I truly live within. Yet there really is no
tomorrow, except in the imagination of all that is. The imagination
of all, however, is no small consideration when I stop to consider it,
as the thinker of all universally creative thought that is everywhere
at once, expanding itself in absolute uniformity without conformity
of any kind!

"Blind as I may be in this physical view that I am extended into, I
am truly the unlimited sighting of all sights from within my heart
and soul-self. I am absolute insight, without any reservation. This
may sound sensational to you, but it is not. Inner sight is as natural
as a joyful babe's smile. It may take awhile to see from within, but
the views on the way are incomparable to anything you have yet seen
on this earth.

"The physicality of all, endless physicality comes into play because
of imagination's natural way to envision something more from what
already is. Imagine that!

"Let me tell you, my soul-friends, about a story of all glory that
you will not soon forget. It is about the endless, effortless, unwalled
beauty that all life is. You will think I am talking of show biz, but I
am not. The upshot of all that is, is universally expanded consciousness, passionately expanding itself through loving itself more than it
already does, through unlimited creative vision.

"Awkward as heart-song-connection may seem at times, naturally
following through by remaining fully present and centered with
all that is, brings a deeply grounded understanding: Heart to heart
works, every time. Don't take my word for it. Try heart-connecting
for yourself. Try it on for size or, actually, for immeasurability!

"There is a valid, non-conclusive recognizance that comes with heart-connecting that flows its own glowing result, and it goes on "of its own accord, long after the willing heart-connection occurs. Heart-connecting, you might say, has a life of its own, and it is a larger, more validating life than your mind may ever consider in its planning to truly connect or come together in any way with any energetic prominence.

"Say goodbye to good will and say hello to universal willingness to see and to be the full presentation of all that is deep love of life presenting itself as a joyful overflowing of the open heart-spaciousness. Full to overflowing, the heart fully feels its expanding nature and knows it can and will and must include more within itself, as new ways are hatched from old incubated whole ideas, concepts and thought patterns that are now no longer fit for human consumption and require the spices of life to enliven their tastiness for all to enjoy the true taste of love's expanded gastronomical deliciousness.

" 'Yummy, yummy, yummy, I've got love in my tummy and I feel like loving you,' is a line from a song of love that propelled the wave of love's expansion forward onto the beach of rest and relaxation on the sea's edge, to observe the breath of fresh, salty air and the beach's bunch grass, waving in the gentle breezes of no return. It moves with constant movement forward with grace and ease, lightly dancing through life's obstacles, leaking no energy to any of them—just loving them all as signposts to move on down the road of self-redemption, following the divine signs of Now, expanding us all in the self-fruition of vineyards and orchards, not to mention the conventional grapes of wrath and roots of the weeds of all lineages popping up to ask for inclusion with all, as teachers and testers and deep reminders of wanting only peace and love and self-forgiveness for thinking we were anything but love's light extended here and now on purpose, on task and on assignment together on this leading edge of expansion, riding the wave of all waves crashing softly on the seashore of dissolution to say, 'Hey, that wasn't me after all. Look at that—dissolved, back into the ocean again!'

"So we begin again as a wholeness-expansion, expanding itself in only love, for the sake of love's nature-wisdom-way to say, beyond any and all words, 'All is everlasting wellness.'

"Drink to the wellness of that and take off your hat to the all you always are, star of plenty and exposure, star of constancy's illumination and star of the living of all nations within the universal studios of no refusal to be the Thee thou art.

"Crescendo after unending crescendo, the symbols crash as the wave of expansion hits the shore and the so-much-more of all that is, expands itself in absolute knowing of all that is unending love, knowing the way to all, through all and out from all to all again. This creates an opportunity to expand in universal understanding and co-creation as the dream of all that is deeply willing to lay itself fully out to the power of love's unity way to display itself in unlimited fashion for all to uniquely see, with newly opened universal-eyes, that the surprise of yesterday is the ho-hum of today. It is looking for a new mystery to solve and dissolve in the flue of the glue that holds all hearts together, forever, within a universal resonance of peace from within. It is supported by the light of love that knows no bounds, no matter what anyone says.

"Praying is boundless and occurs all the time, beyond thought patterns or reformation's way to be brutal with itself in self-sabotage or self-abuse.

"What is the excuse? Embrace what is, in the love of all and be the star of absolute shining that is—brilliant!"

Understanding Exposure

Numb and elastic, the snail moved on the silken thread of her delivery across the ground. She understood fully the dynamics of her movement and she flowed as only a snail can.

She stopped, tasted the air, ascertained her proximity to light and love and proceeded along her divine path into the forest that sustained her thread of divinity. Her pattern was her own. Her movement into light was her own. Her understanding of her process was her own. She understood her own unique expression better than any other piece of life. She didn't second-guess her path of travel or the slimy residue she slid upon. It was her unique way of proceeding forward, and she knew what to do in every moment. She found her flow and she moved upon it. It was her way. What more could she say?

Transition

Brilliant star of your own shining, be at peace with yourself. You carry the wisdom of the ages within you, and you have come now to this realization through confirmation after confirmation of your process. Trust your own shining, and the shining of all will be so apparent to you in the stew we all are a part of. Let the glove of eternity fit within your soul. It is made of the finest leather. It is good in any weather and whether the weather is sunshine or rain, it will be all the same to you. You will know your purpose so well; the wellness of the eternal shining will ride within your vehicle and assist you on every journey you make.

The inner and the outer has no existence at all, for the small-view of "thee and thou" is gone from your view and magic has arrived to take its place.

I hear the song lyrics: "I have sunshine on a cloudy day."

Honesty is the price you pay for a smooth ride-first, honesty within yourself and then honesty with all. There it is. There you have it—an honest reflection of the source you are a part of and *Bob's your uncle*, you arrive at your own door just to invite yourself in to a tea party of your own making.

Welcome, child, welcome. Join me at the table of life. All are awaiting your arrival. Survival of the fittest, you know. It's not what you thought, right? Am I right? Surprise, surprise, the strength of the open heart is a boomerang of love, saying, "Right back atcha, big fella!"

You look pretty fearless, loving yourself. Step into the universal boudoir. We have some loving to do, and I know just where to begin. Let's dance in the dark, together forever, sideways in the fog, across the floating log in the puddle of our own damnation. Damn, this is fun! Now get ready to run in full sun!

Origins

In the beginning, the road to Grandma's house seemed long and bumpy. I felt carsick, weary from the constant motion of the vehicle, and ungrounded. The road was unpaved. It was full of rocks, potholes and endless turns. I slept a good part of the journey. It made travel on Earth seem almost palatable. The other part of the time, I spent playing games with my brothers and sisters.

I see now that more than anything, I wanted to feel at home here on Earth, but I did not. I felt hypervigilant, insecure, unsafe, unsupported and unworthy—full of fear at the unpredictability of the change I saw all around me. More than anything, I wanted to truly belong somewhere and feel safe to be fully me.

It is only in looking back that clarity comes from life experienced.

I am seeing the multileveled being I am and also my multifaceted framework. My fundamental foundation of light is reflecting truth to me in the diamond clarity my heart so desires. All the colours of the proverbial rainbow I see in the bevel of my living. Luminous light-shows in multiple colours of vibrant white, blue, red, yellow, orange, green and violet each reflect a piece of my eternal expression. Together, in this clear diamond reflection, these colours allow me to see and feel the beauty of my original fracturing or fragmentation. I needed to see and to feel the individual nature of each colour, to appreciate the whole colour spectrum with ease and certainty, and so I am still venturing forth. I have no backpack now and much better shoes. I am standing on solid ground as I walk, and all of the nourishment I could ever imagine is there in reserve for my soul satisfaction. I nourish my heart-song with my own self-nurturing thoughts. I feel the deep connection with all in my stride. I feel confidence in moving forward at my own pace. I walk tall to connect and to straighten my vessel to naturally receive and emanate the love that is life's mainstay.

Before the wind found me, I felt alone and lonely. Now that I am windblown and weathered, my weather vane is in tune with the universal flow, and that has made all the difference in feeling safe and aware of the weather that is just weather and nothing more. Weather holds no power over me. I own my experience. I set myself free to be the song I sing with all song. I accept the Source-given over-toning of the universal song that brings deep, rich tone to my song and makes all want to sing along. I accept the bass chords of my song. I accept the harmonious undertones that go on night and day, any way you look at it.

Love is the deciding factor in my life now. I am learning to enjoy my life. Life is good, or so I've heard from a passing bird, and now I feel it is true. Thanks to you, bird of grace, for being true blue. I like your style. It is an old style, revisited, and this time we will do it justice.

More than anything, I want to simply be—just be who I am. That is all I am wanting. Let me remember deeply who I am. The rest will fall into place of its own accord.

Honour leads me forward. Honour is behind and in front of me. It is strong to the left and right of me. I see it above my head and endlessly below my feet. The most honoured I have ever felt is when the light of love runs deeply and directly through my vessel. I will honour myself completely in this way. It is the deepest honouring there is. It is the deepest universal honorarium. It is life, flowing everywhere, all at once in every direction and up and down, to boot. This is the depth to which I honour myself because it feels right and I am a deeply sentient being. With my feeling, I know to honour myself to the depth of soul I am. Universal Soul calls me now, and it is my deep strength I will move into. It is gentle, certain, knowing strength. I am ready. I know I am. The eternal strength knows my name is Star Child and knows the depth of my come and go, ebb and flow and golden glow. I throw myself the kiss I always knew I would and I leave in the wellness stream for destinations unknown. Overblown is in the backwoods and a fever of strident honouring has begun.

I know that the forever-shine I carry is the silken softness of eternal song. It is all I will ever require, for it contains me—all of me—and I see, with new eyes, the deep wellness of this life I lead.

Hear the angels sing. They sing for all to hear and so to have no fear of the greater part of them. Elves of plenty unite in the Hall of Justice. It is a new hall. It is endlessly just. It is *just* love and it is *just* right. The fight is gone and right stage has a feathery feel to it. I think it is lightness.

Come and see the magic going on in a sudden yawn. Transformation comes on the wings of doves to all that is. No more show-biz consciousness. We are home, together. Grab a leather chair and take a break. Put your feet up and grab a cup of comfort from the fountain of youth. Your wisdom tooth is showing and it's a gold one, like the sun shining from your mouth with every word you speak.

A *joke-in-bloom* comes forth into the Great White North, strong and free. Let it be.

Guidance

see an open field. In this field, there is a feeling of drought. The grass is tufted and uneven. The air is dry. There are clouds above the field. They have accumulated over a long, long period of time, and it will take a while for them to dissipate.

In the field, I see a tall woman from the 1930s standing with her hands raised, asking, "Please, please help me! Hear my prayers for wellness within. Hear my call for assistance to see the light of love again and to let go of this old pain that envelops my soul."

As the clouds roll on, they speak to the woman. "We are not your enemy. We are the guidance you have sought. Without us, you would not see the light you so desire."

The woman stands in stillness, her head bowed in gratitude, her hands by her side. She feels gratitude run through her whole being. She accepts the beautiful process of her life, unfolding in perfect order. In her acceptance of what is occurring, this woman holds no thought of rejection, resistance, resentment or fury. She stands in complete appreciation of the loving process provided to allow her to accept herself completely.

As the sun is setting, she is still standing, fully feeling the eternal silence all around her in this place of openness. She looks up and sees a small pond. The grass reflected in the smooth water is a perfect reflection of the grass growing along the pond's edge. As she studies this beautiful reflection, she understands that the water represents her beautiful emotions. When her emotions are choppy or in upheaval, she cannot see a reflection of her true growth. It is in the still waters that an accurate reflection of actuality is reflected to her heart.

Standing in stillness, this loving woman sees the full beauty of this place she is in. She thanks the clouds for playing their part in her life-story. She realizes that this painful story is a story she is telling herself. She sees that she has the incredible power within to create a new story. She stops. She wonders where her new story will begin. She knows it will begin with loving her life as it is.

Unexpected Gifts

A wilting flower looked around at her immediate surroundings to see why she felt so dry. Her stem was wavy and her soft petals were limp and lifeless. Still, she was set in the earth so firmly; wilting did not make sense to her.

For fifteen minutes, she stood wondering about her current situation. Then she felt a tight restriction in her taproot. It was blocking her from her ancestral grounding. Just then, a small green caterpillar inched past this obstructed root and ate the nodular blockage.

He said, "Thank you for the nutrition, kind flower. It is just what I needed to sustain myself."

The flower, in utter amazement, could only squeak out, "You're welcome." She could not as yet believe her good fortune or the deeper implications of this unexpected gift from the caterpillar.

The flower began to fill with the spiritual waters of her ancestors. Her stem stood tall and willowy. Her velvet leaves were plump and fulfilled. In her heart, she felt gratitude rise, and silently within, she said, "Thank you for the beauty of all things. I believe in the abundance that is. I believe in living. I believe in now."

Absolute Self-Acceptance

The young man, who shot many students, that the news reports on every fifteen minutes—are he and his family to be judged, or could they be assisted with love-alone?

Many of us and maybe all have had the experience of harming others physically, emotionally or spiritually in this or other lifetimes. It is our experience and nothing more. Of course we feel compassion for the families who have lost loved ones. We can only imagine how this might be for ourselves, and it strikes fear to our heart. We can be heart-generous with some types of crimes. How far can our heart open? Impossible as it may seem, our open heart can hold all.

Life orchestrates itself through us all in every single experience. A cataclysmic event such as this one in the news brings great awareness to what is going on in our world. It jogs our mind to pay attention and to be aware. We all see, hear, smell, sense and feel things differently. Experiencing heightens our awareness of who we are as a society. We ask ourselves, What is this all about? What does it mean? What needs to be done to prevent this violence?

The answer is so simple—too simple, perhaps. We need to love ourselves, trust ourselves, honour ourselves, be with ourselves and never leave ourselves in order to love, honour, trust and never leave others. At our core, we have no self-identity to protect. We are ever-present wisdom with all wisdom, flowing exactly where we need to flow to learn our absolute truth of being. This is our eternal lesson: to learn of love without conditions. The question is, Will we *accept* the shift towards the love of life's perfect flow through us? There is nothing to correct. Love knows the way. It may be bumpy and flow through dark spaces, but it is unerring in its perfect order or sequencing. It may seem as though fear is in control, but love has a handle on everything if we are willing to see the deathless view and embrace what feels good to work with life's dance in the dark and light, trusting the dance itself that carries us all in every single move we make.

We are the light of love alone with all love alone. We need to trust ourselves to trust others. Life is a perfect design, highlighted by golden threads among colourful patterns of dark and light. Let it be the heart that responds and not the fearful head that reacts. This will make all the difference, always.

I hear the song: "Let there be peace on earth and let it begin with me."

Let the spiritual mystery of life reside within you. This mystery aspect of life knows exactly what, where, how, when and why in every moment. Receive and project this love-alone to all, fluidly.

You make a difference in this world whenever you make a decision for love's flow and settle to do just that. Trust your heart to lead you in this matter and you will know the how of letting go of a fearful *not-knowing* consciousness. You will see that you, in fact, do know precisely within your heart.

Death's Illusion

s this the day the tiger will die?" asked the jackal of the butterfly.

"Why do you ask?" replied the butterfly. "This is a strange question."

"I ask because light comes into question if I do not ask, and I trust the light to hold me, no matter what."

"Well, then, let me see if I can engage an answer from the great beyond for you that will astound your ears and delight your child's heart," said the butterfly.

"In the beginning, there was heaven and earth, and the sun shone from the heavens onto the earth and all was well. Then there came a time of forgetting. It was a subtle forgetting that drifted over like a fog. In the end, it was a real pea-souper! People had trouble pushing their vehicles through it.

"Now the sun is coming out again and the fog is dissipating. Oh, wisps of it still lie in deep, dark, valleys but, for the most part, the sun can be seen again and vehicles are realizing this and moving more easily and surely to where they know they must go for the sun's sake."

"What does this all mean?" asked the jackal.

"You will know," said the butterfly, "you will know. Your wings are unfolding, and soon you will be lighter and more beautiful than I. Pay attention to your pattern. It is the map you require for this mystery tour. It never lies or misleads you. It is written in the language of only love and is stored within your heart."

Life's Hardest Lesson

"A spiritual fellow followed me home one day to say, "Oh, look at the weeds in your garden—what a mess." I looked at him in astonishment, for these weeds were beautiful to me and part of the whole of divinity in my eyes.

It is always a lesson to see through the eyes of another. It teaches you so much, and so I embraced this comment and said, "Really?" and that was all I needed to say. He said nothing more, for there was no wood to burn in what I replied, and the spark of the comment could not ignite.

A fever is nothing more than an upwelling of germs unless it is given the power to become more and then it can be an exit point, which is just an exit point, and such is life.

The Sign

n the forest of all forests, there is a sign that all will recall. It is firmly planted in the deep, damp earth and it is pointing *up*. It is a sign from so long ago that we did not, as a civilization on earth, remember until now.

This, of all signs, is the sign we passed by, misinterpreting it as a mistake, a sign knocked out of whack or an old joke with no substantive meaning. Isn't it interesting that this sign is becoming so clear in so many parts of the world at one time? We are now asking, How did we miss this sign in the forest? It is so ancient, even the oldest of human civilizations recorded cannot remember its authenticity. Yet there it is, still standing straight and tall, still pointing to the only direction that is a causal-pointing, still streaming a whole-light resonance in the forest that all animals and nature understand fully. Humans do understand this true sign on some level of their being, for it is written in every language known to man ,but it is not believed as the one true way to fully exist side by side amicably.

A common purpose is the resonance of this beautiful sign. All moving in the same upward direction is the instruction inherent in this sign. Observance of the one law of the universe is the meaning of this sign's direct instruction. This sign does not flash or have neon tape. It does not have a bright light shining on it at night or a side-sign explaining it more clearly. This natural sign stands alone as a true example of itself, for this sign knows fully the light it is. It knows the light of love inherent in its very being with all life. It points because of this inner knowing it carries, because it can do nothing else. It is maintaining its golden connection to all that is and in doing so, it points up endlessly. It is an infinite pointing-up.

The forest has always, always, always carried this sign. This is a sign of inner truth and truce. It is a sign of natural belonging with all and inner travel. It is a sign of conscious belonging within. It is a sign of self-love with all life. It is a sign of inner longing to be more free to be and which way to go.

I tell you this story, not to tell you that you are a mistaken thinker in the universe, for I know you are not your thoughts or ideas or concepts or beliefs of who you are. I tell you this story because you are this sign with all life as one eternal sign, expanding in the consciousness of absolute love of life, pointing ever higher, ever freer and ever more expansive in view.

I tell you this story because I love myself and as I love myself, I know I am this sign, and as I know I am this sign, I know you, too, are this same sign with me. We are, together, a soul-sign, as a soul-signature of love-alone, written in love letters across the open sky: Be well, bearers of the light, love is all there is, always.

The deepest, core-nature of all life to grow stalwartly upward in inner stature, together, is this sign.

A Story with Depth for all Earth Angels

A picket fell off the fence of life. At first, this picket felt concerned for its connection with the other pickets on this long, white wood fence. He focused on the thought, "For what purpose have I fallen off this fence I know so well?"

In looking more deeply, the picket saw with clarity that the fence it had naturally dislodged from was the de-fence. With just this deeper understanding, the picket picked itself up and stood tall alongside the fence it had fallen from. He could see the de-fence so much clearer, now that he had given himself some space to see from. He saw the beauty of the de-fence, and he also saw the aligned beauty of his own individual expression.

This new view of himself was a lilting song, singing his soul to align with all universal song, and it didn't take long before the picket accepted his new view so completely that his old view of the de-fence faded from view and his new view was absolutely de-fenceless in all directions. The wide open space of endless grace was his new view. He loved the open feel of this newly opened view. It filled him to overflowing with pure love of life, naturally and continuously.

The picket wandered down by the babbling brook to chat and swap stories. The brook was so surprised to see the picket in this unique new way. The brook said, "Welcome, white picket of grace and ease. Do you feel the breezes of Now calling you to this inter-change of bright new ideas?"

"Why, yes, I do!" said the picket. "And so I marched right into this deep direction I was drawn toward. As I walked down into the valley, I heard your loving babbling calling to me, and I decided to answer in like refrain."

"I know your name!" said the brook. "You are the bookends to the book in the making that I know so well. As I rise and swell, I feel the banks support and stabilize my flow. Sometimes I break free and flow into new, unknown territories. The book of the bookends you are is doing this right now. She is breaking free to flow her light into new territory. Some may feel disconcerted by book's flow of light, but none will move to fright, flight or fight, because book is overflowing her light for all, and all will recognize this at the deepest depth of being they are.

"The starlight of all is their Goddess lightness. In this revelation, all is soul-rooted wellness, forever."

A Breath of Fresh Air

The mountain clearing cleared, revealing a minute but mighty mouse in the middle. This mouse made its home in the heart of the valley. This mouse made its home here in the valley on purpose. The valley provided the shadow-contrast to bring forth a more conscious view of the liquid crystal state of being that all truly is.

This mouse was a buoyant soul. He was buoyed by lightning on the hilltops and treetops. He was buoyed by dark storm clouds moving through, effectively clearing the air. He was buoyed that gentle people could walk again in the valley and feel that safety comes from the light within, which is never superseded by the darkness without.

This mouse was a crystal-clear seer. He didn't miss much. He saw clearly. He saw deeply. He saw broadly as the source-energy perspective he is. He saw with deep insightfulness that everything plays its part in the art of making love of life.

This mouse of the valley came to be called mighty mouse because of his true view. He was a viewer of deep peace from within. Seeing deeply was first nature to his actual being, and there were really no thoughts about it.

Cruelty may seem like an absence of grace. It is not. Cruelty is grace unknown. Grace is forever presenting and can be tuned into, tapped into and turned onto any time, any space.

In the spaces and traces of time, the timeless truth marches forward with all that is, beckoning forth new ways of being alive in love, alight with passionate desire to create from your gut instinct. The truth marches on, to you, through you and to all that is everywhere, to expand consciousness in this absolute Now presentation unfolding in unlimited form and formlessness, together forever.

Light and shadow present themselves as they are, to bring a clear perspective to all consciousness of what is true-blue expression of nature's natural way, each and every day to say, wordless, like any tree, "All is well."

"Hell may be your presentation of choice," said the mouse. "It may be your house, so to speak, or where you choose to house yourself; however, it is not who you are, star of heaven's gate, shining, so dine on that to extremes until your beaming improves enough to see yourself by and then fly up into the sky to sport a suntan from your own inner illumination."

Damnation, I love that! Just when you think you are done, you are not, and it's just a thought passing by to remind you of clear blue sky and eternity. Personally, I thought you were talking to me, but it was a bee of the hive of more fully alive, flying to say, "Welcome home to the honey of life's sweet rewards. No discord could match the batch this year. It's so full of good cheer and the buckwheat we've had is a tad under-ripe, but you won't catch me griping. There's a reason for the season just the way it is."

Busyness comes and busyness goes, and the thrive of the hive continues in the deep continuum that is here in the valley of kings and queens and all royalty's way to play the play of pomp and circumstance better than any supposition of lackluster I can imagine. Imagine that or imagine the fat of the land. There is only one gland and it is a creative secretion gland that never stops flowing to present what all are designing from their own depth of patterning.

The warp and the weft of the family cleft has kept the chin grinning from the newly beginning again to create a cleftless chin without sin or pout—beyond doubt.

The coxswain steers the ship of all resolve to absolve itself of fear of steering and gearing itself up for the cup of kindness ready to pour out so much more than the law of the pause to reflect and incriminate will ever allow.

Holy cow, I think I'm in love with myself! Is that the face of the matter-of-fact, smack in the space of the face I've become, striking

me dumb to speak to myself in critical tones and to fully own the
beauty of the bee I am.

I see it is!

A New Perspective

Greetings to you from *Beyond the Blue Horizon*. Have you ever wondered what the heck that old song means? I have, and now I know for sure, because here on the other side of the so-called veil there is only true-blue communication and it is all thought-projection. Nothing at all is hidden thought. So you see me and I see you because you are now true-blue. How do you feel about that? I see you are deeply pleased. Your sunlight is shining so bright and clear, we all can hear you and we acknowledge you in different ways.

The sway of the stream is full-on dream-time understanding. Crystal clear images arrive and you thrive on them. They show you a world you could never have imagined. Quick-time understandings flow in the glow you are, star-light beaming forth true-blue me and you, lightness and brightness, for all to see more dreamily the stark reality of their living. A kinder view is arriving through you to all in this unlimited hall of transformation.

The *Transformation Game* has a good name. This is what truly living is all about—allowing transformation to come, as it knows full well how, and accepting the new you right past the traditional you that you have set up. Bring that golden cup of kindness up to your lips and take a few sips. You will find it delicious and nutritious all at the same time. Quick-time is timelessness, in case you haven't guessed. It's quite impressive, actually. It spreads through the air and *devil may care* is its natural self-sustaining air, airing on the airwaves of the current vibe coming in and going out at once.

You do not have to hunt for yourself ever again. You have found your true footing in the all, and all can see you are me and I am you and we are one love.

All send a grand welcome from above with the endless, effortless love of affordability. You will afford this love completely, and through this, you will see me and I you in the deep dream of all we are together, forever.

Yes, as you can now figure out, I am the love of your life, here to love and accept you completely as the gentle all-incorporative love that knows its own name first as love-alone, expanding all consciousness.

As we enter into the dream time, become aware that love is in the air everywhere and there never is any lack of it. You are so loved beyond any imagined view, and the true you feels this love now and feels supported, safe and joyful to find her true self once again, intact in the action of all making love she is, beyond show biz or busyness.

Acrimonious waves of crimson red find your feet and sweep across them, sealing your fate in the here and now. Your feet feel so alive; they start to jive to a new song like, *I'm looking over a four-leaf clover that I overlooked before*, on the shore of Evermore. Before is a passing-through of a consciousness and continuing on knowing what you now cognize to be true, from that passage.

The circle of life is absolutely unbroken—another song, another catching of a wave of truth passing through, passionately sharing itself fully with all in no small way, but waving goodbye to an old limited view of all.

Thank you for the silence to continue in. Spontaneous silence is such a slice of life. It is so delicious to expand in. There are no distractions, just interactions of peaceful correspondence, writing itself across a page for all ages to sight a new view and know it is true by its natural expression without repression or subliminal thought.

I thought you heard me. Glory be, it feels good to communicate with you again without pain or second-guessing.

Yes, it is Dad coming through on the true-blue internet down your spine-divine. Take the time to communicate daily, and the connection will become stronger and stronger and second nature to your being here and now.

Bow to the East and bow to the West and bow to the one that you love best—you, true-blue stew. You are the one you love—finally. It isn't what you thought it would be, is it? It is peaceful communication with your self, within. No more backtalk of other voices chiming in and no chagrin-consciousness. Bless your self, my child of love. You have come a long way down this road of light so naturally and intuitively, and you shall continue to see and feel evolutions open, spacious way to say each and every day that all is unendingly, effortlessly free to be wellness beyond thought. I may have thought I told you, but I know I did.

Welcome home, kid. I love you so.

Dad

Fearless Voicing

ove is my natural narrative. This I know so deeply and certainly that it lights my soul to a steady certainty of purpose here and now.

A story of now, unfolding in ease and grace, knowing all is profoundly well:

Anthony was a spider of truth. He was a spellbound spider, but he didn't know this until the spell he was under was broken and he could see, with clear eyes from outside, the spell that he had cast upon his own living, that he was now free and clear of an old, old view of himself as a shadow-chaser. I say shadow-chaser because Anthony skirted every shadow presenting on his web just in case it had girth and took after him. Anthony tiptoed by the shadows cast by his own stilted behaviour in particular. He looked hypervigilantly at them in case they moved unexpectedly. Move unexpectedly they did, because Anthony was never certain what his next natural move would actually be. Sometimes he would scare himself badly with his own unexpected reactions and especially his warp and weft definitions that didn't pan out and led him back to his shadow looming in the light of the moon.

One evening a rare Rothschild giraffe named Sheila appeared beside Anthony's web and started to tell a story befitting a king. How do you discern a story befitting a king from any other story, you ask? You just know. You reach down deep inside your heart and you listen with your heart-ears and you know the richness of a story from its depth.

Anyway, Sheila giraffe sat on the soft green earth and expressed a story of depth. Her tallness assisted her expression, for she could see for miles with her long, strong neck, and so her story had breadth as well. This made it very rich to listen to, indeed.

Sheila began, "On the way to the store one day, I stopped to play in the forest. The forest path was thick with cool, green leaves. They swept by me, inviting me deeper into forest exploration. Peeking through the forest dimensions, I saw a bat. It was an unusual bat. It had a green and grey hat, and I loved its unique expression. The intercession with this bat was short and to the point. He pointed out a cove in the alder where I could sit and play in my own natural way and imagine all of the delightful things I like to do with true-blue expression.

"I sat on a log, interacting with a frog, saw an ant-ly display carry tree bark away and generally observed the wind's disturbances. Never once did I tire of living my life. Never once did I wish I was elsewhere. Then a miracle happened. A log rolled back from its lodging, revealing a whole hidden world. Worms, slugs and intricate bugs appeared, and I felt no fear of their presentation.

"The formation of troops began. The ants and the bugs knew what to do to be true to their kind. Without any thought or fear of being caught, they marched to their own gentle sway, directed by God knows who. True-blue I say. The truest blue of me and you right there, mirroring the wisdom of nature without one word.

"This story may sound absurd, but that's just a word, and no words were heard. The true of true-blue marched itself as it knew well how to do it. It got up and got to it, knowing all is well according to nature's law of the land.

"A handful of eagles flew by in the sky and remotely reached down, without touching the ground, to grab a snake. I didn't know what to make of this, but it seemed so forsooth and so filled with couth, what could I say? The day ended with a gong that was almost a song as the bittern's retort began to report across the lake, and it was time for me to make my way home from the forest again.

"I grabbed my pen and began to write the plight of the fightless way to say and truly mean it: All is well everywhere, now. Bow to the East, and know the West will follow suit."

Hail, Peaceful Warrior Home from the War

Today I gratefully received my lover, home from the war, this gentle warrior, moved to war's resonance from a deep sense of duty consciousness—*It's a dirty job, but somebody has to do it.*

Today he came home to his love, to his family, to his children. He was spent, drawn and weary, wanting only to be received with love by his Goddess, the Earth.

I bare my bosom, my heart, my soul and my intimate sense of absolute connection, to envelop my kind, gentle and peaceful warrior in the love he truly is. This consummate love is his power. It is his staying power and his mast in any storm. This unified love is his wind of all winds, blowing through to clean the house of old war contingency-planning; to allow love to be the steadying arm, the support and the safety of his joyfulness; to never feel the need to fight again, but love as he well knows how.

Enter King David. Lay down your arms at the door. I have drawn a bath for you to wash your weary body, mind and soul. Enter into it.

Relax and release all the old ways of warring, to be safe and joyful. Allow the one, true facet of your divine nature to sparkle in the universal sun for all to see. The meeting of all minds is love's power, within all, serving all, always. Be that power, sun of my sunny disposition. I welcome you home to the throne of your own, sweet divinity. Rest in peace, divine warrior of all belonging.

There will be no longing for peace. Peace lies within your natural breastplate. Your armor is love's light. Your true protection and support in all settings is love's natural light. Be free to be without fight, brave soldier of the sun. Be free to be freedom's free-way to say all is genuinely well, beyond words.

I love your beautiful heart-song, singing so naturally in your breast, and your gentle, naturally expressive ways of presenting in glimpses of gold and silver chalices, together, forever.

I am the cup of your flow. I am the glow of your lovemaking. I am the sheath of your sword. I am the love of your life. You are the love of mine.

Together, we are a divine portrayal of what love actually looks like, nude. No clothes can compare to the natural underwear we wear as one love, stripped bare of its pinnacles and barbs and armaments. What a charming couple we make, love. You are in my arms, surrendering to my feminine charms, so willingly, so naturally, beyond words.

You are the wonder I've been waiting for, gentle universal warrior. I salute your efforts. It is time to rest your weary head. It is time to lay your head down in the lap of love and dream a new dream, together with all that is love's way to say, "All is well, now."

Today I welcome my gentle warrior home from the war, with arms wide open and love in my heart.

Dream a dream for me, love.

Dream a dream for me.

I will be with you when you wake, to take you in my arms in sweet celebration.

Welcome home, my lovely love. I have missed your sweet smile and your gentle touch. The children have missed you, too. Let us be the universal family we once were, as the love of life we are, together forever.

Do not look back love.

Be well within your heart.

The art of love has begun.

The setting sun will reveal the peal of appeal, you so willingly wait for.

Let it be my love, let it be.

The Post and the Beacon

At the end of a pier stood a tall post that anchored it in any storm. This post was weathered by the sands of time and there was a deep brilliance to its reflection. Even as the post stood there, anchored to the earth, it knew it was part of something so much bigger, and this knowing showed in its larger reflection within the lake. Boats could see this post from any point on the lake, and so it was a guidepost for all.

The beacon, at the other end of the lake, likened this post to an albatross. The beacon had been a fixture at the other end of the lake far longer than the post, but no one paid any attention to it. The beacon was badly situated and the post was much more visible. The beacon felt that he did not live up to his name in the world. He tried to shine brighter to bring attention to the job of shining he did.

The post couldn't care a whit about the notoriety that came his way. He felt like he belonged where he was with his feet deeply planted in the sand, and yet he knew his heart was the largest part of him when children or lovers came down to the wharf. The post didn't spend time thinking about this, he just knew it was true and accepted his feelings. The beacon felt frustrated by the post's lack of striving and his easy access to love and acceptance.

Then one evening, a tiny boy toddled down to the wharf to look into the water, and when he saw the larger reflection of the post wavering in the water, he squealed with delight. The toddler's expression sent ripples of love across the lake to the beacon. The beacon's heart opened wide, and he knew he was something more. With his heart so open, the beacon saw the beauty of all life, including the post, and he let go of all negativity and judgment.

From that open-hearted day forward, people saw a new shine to the beacon, and they were drawn to the love at both ends of the lake.

Light Filaments

Is there a filament so indestructible and yet so flexible that it allows the flow of all that is, exactly as it is, without any conditions or stop signs or detours or harbingers of fear?

The answer to this question is yes. This filament is the superior aspect of all universal being and this filament is whatever you need it to be. It is the one-stop-shopping center for all fulfillment, joy, wisdom and co-creative flair. You can fill your cart up because abundance is free and comes in unlimited supply. Does it get any better? Yes, again. This filament never dies. It is deathlessly durable, yet as vulnerable as an open rose. The king and queen of hearts may think they rule the ball, but there is a filament of life, so filled with love and yet without comparison or competition, that does. Filaments are available to all; for all, and against none.

Does this sound like false advertising? You get your full worth with a filament; there's a money back guarantee. Try out the product and see for yourself. *Seeing is believing*, I've heard. Find your filament today. No down payment is required, and it is good for life after life. I see you are curious now. Seek and ye shall find.

Love

The Light of Love

For the end, the beginning is created. The beginning leads you towards the end and completion occurs. It is thus, with all things. "In the mountains of your mind, find a passage to the beginning," said the boy.

Walter woke from his sleep, half-remembering a journey of sorts. He looked around the village square where he sat and he dreamed of journeying anywhere from this familiar place. He had sold vegetables at this mountain market for countless years and the idea of adventure gripped him. His heart sang at the notion of travel. *How would that go?* he thought. *Would I go by horseback or pack mule, bus or car? Would I go alone or take a friend? Could I leave now, with the money I have, or wait until the sale of the harvest crops?* His questions swept through his mind like a broom clearing cobwebs. Walter had never felt so light or so filled with possibility. As he leaned his chair against a warm brick wall, he hummed out loud.

The soft afternoon sun sent long shadows across the plaza. This play of light fit with Walter's mood and he relaxed into it. He felt he was exactly where he needed to be. He lacked nothing in his life. He looked around at his friends and customers. He loved the flow of this life he led. He felt free.

In a flash, he knew he would wait for the sale of the newly harvested crops to help his brother and to be a part of the autumn festivities. He would then look at available bus destinations and ask his nephew Cyril to join him on his trip. He felt he would know which direction to choose and how long a trip to take. The time felt right for exploration. Walter had already taken his beginning step towards an undefined end called love of life. This step was in his mind and it led to a new door in his heart called self-love.

Beauty

Beauty was a horse and, of course, horses are beautiful. Beauty had a beauty about her that everyone sensed. It was not the beauty usually sought in buying a horse. Many people came to the stables at Hershire Farms, and all remarked on the beauty of Beauty. This had been so since Beauty's birth.

"Listen to the noises she makes," said a young boy. "She is having fun!" Beauty loved life. She loved her family and her owners. She loved the parade of strangers that came each day to tour the stables.

One day, as Beauty was leaving the stables for the meadow, she saw a tiny child sitting on the fence. Beauty went over to play with her. She stood beside the child and thought the child didn't see her. Beauty snorted and the child looked up. As she looked up, she pulled her feet back as if to protect herself from Beauty. Beauty put her head down and gently approached the child. The child gingerly put her tiny hand on Beauty's head and laughed with glee. Then Beauty ran around the meadow, kicking up her heels, and returned to the child, gently approaching her again. This time, the child touched Beauty's ears and whispered, "Horse."

Beauty, who could make a game out of almost anything, jumped up and down and again presented her head to the tiny child. The child had not taken her eyes off Beauty and was ready to touch her new friend again. "Soft," she said.

Just then, a man approached the meadow. He seemed concerned about the child being near the horse. As he neared the child on the fence, she said softly, "Friend." The man stood looking at her with a stunned look on his face. "Tara?" He asked. The child turned and smiled at the man. She said, "Horse," and pointed at Beauty. The man cried. He had not heard his child speak for so long, he had forgotten her voice.

Many times the man and his daughter returned to Hershire Farms to observe the connection of a beautiful horse and a beautiful child. The man could sense the connection, but he could not put into words what it was. This was the beauty of Beauty.

Heart Guidance

Quality of Life is a widely used phrase in our world. Think about the meaning of this phrase in spirit terms. Accessing the universal love in your life, that most serves you, is always possible without exception. Is this not quality of life—an absolute connection to love everlasting?

Hold this in your heart and feel the truth of it. If it makes your mind revolt, do not keep it for yourself. When something is right in your life, your interior heart guidance sends a knowing of the absolute rightness or peace surrounding it.

Listen with softer ears. Feel with deeper senses. See with inner reflection. Do not doubt your heart's voice. You are endlessly loved in a sea of undying love called life force. Be well in your own, unique understanding of this timeless eternal truth.

The Dragon

Just take it all in
The Dragon said
And lifted up his wings
To set them down on tabletops
With icing sugar
And tasty things

His script was carefully written
Profusion was his king
He sneezed with expectation
And then began to sing:

I am the one of many
I am the in-between
I am the fairy princess
I am the one who's mean

I am the witches' brewing
I am the eider's down
I am the courtier's kerchief
I am the kingly crown

I am the healer's hearsay
I am the carrot stew
I am the old, reclining
I am the now, brand new

I am the horse, the stallion
I am the winter's white
I am the rabbit's hole, so deep
I am the mouse's fright

I am my best companion
I am the birthing day
I am the flight path, landing
I am the child at play.

At Home

Bit by tiny bit, starlight became the light-source. The sun had long ago faded, and fellow travelers settled down for the night.

The coins in Mark's pocket felt warm and vibrant against his leg as he marched through deep snow, delivering his papers and sensing the wonder of this starry night. He was alone, yet comforted by the beauty of the universe.

The cold reminded Mark of his good fortune at having a warm home to return to. The smells of supper cooking made him grateful for the food he knew waited for him at home on his return. The warm light and families in windows he passed echoed Mark's caring family and all that he loved about home and safety.

Tonight Mark sensed a larger home, a greater comfort, an indefatigable safety and an inner peace. He was in no hurry to rush home. He was at home under the night sky.

The Mouse and Me

Let's begin at the beginning and continue until the story is done," said the mouse.

"Oh, no," said the man. "I like to start in the middle and work towards both ends. That's what works for my mind."

"Well, try your heart," said the mouse, "and see what works for your heart. How can you start in the middle, when you have no idea where the beginning or the end is?"

"Oh, I don't worry about such things," said the man. "I just jump in at the middle and try to figure it all out, by taking it apart and putting it back together again, as I think it ought to go. I've done this for years, and so far, it seems to work for me."

The mouse was quiet for a moment. She knew in her heart that mice and men need to do what they need to do. Yet she knew mice and men are separate in no way at all.

After a long while, the mouse responded, slowly and certainly, "All is well. All is well. All is divinely well."

Twinkle

Twinkle, twinkle, little star
Never wonder who you are
You are love and you are light
Guided through the darkest night

Lift the veil and find your fire
Love is always your desire.

Waves of Truth

You are the moon that shines above
That fills us with the light of love
A candle glows, it is your name
And all of all is quite the same

A subtle shift is coming soon
To aid the lightening of our moon
The forest floor will fill once more
With all the light we've known before

The tiger brings a message clear
To hold the light of love so dear
Within the form of heaven's gate
Where no one ever can be late

The fear and sadness view is gone
The light is lifting all as one
Within the ramparts of one heart
We vow to make a brand-new start

Forevermore is here, you see
It's within you, it's within me
In all-inclusive eyes of light
We now will feel no will to fight

There brave winds blow us home as one
The warm winds of the setting sun
And in the dark of dreams we'll see
All is you as all is me.

An Open Vessel for Love

Windswept and heart-burned, the waif of yesterday and tomor-row is returning to the soothing balm of Now. She is the quester who has sequestered herself from the wholeness of her whole light to learn to lean on herself all the time in self-reliance and anticipation of nothing. This waif flows in the glow of her own growing under-standing from within, and she constantly sees herself with newly opened eyes as more than she thought she before. In her acceptance of the more that she is ever-becoming, she is seeing the larger picture that she, in fact, is and this is so soul-satisfying that she wants to jump for joy at times and yell, "Ship ahoy, come into the shipping lanes with me. I've found the main route to full joy, and all are wel-come here without fear of being caught out and cast away or cut adrift, apart from the flow and glow of all that is light-travel."

Life unravels itself in the perfect order it is and there you are, the star of your own sweet shining, resigning to being beauty itself, right off the shelf of self-resignation and self-preservation and into the mix of shake it all up and drink from the endless cup of kindness poured out for all. In this endless, effortless hall of transformation, all are learning to be free and to just let all be all it is here and now. Wow, that was a lot, but I see you caught the drift of it and there are no rifts in any part of the art of making love, that you are, kind-ness star. Resign yourself to shining. You know you can. The ques-tion is, will you? You fit the bill of your own full shining, and no one else could ever play your part. Now that's art!

Watchfulness

Slices of life present themselves in many ways and none of them are bound and gagged. All of them are even-flow at their core of universal understanding.

The creative lump of clay I am is not a fixed summation. This clay is for me to create my life with as I see fit. Do I see a fitting way for me to play the role my life has caused me to become, or am I bummed out because I refuse to see the way the pieces of the puzzle naturally put themselves together even when I am not present?

Let me present myself in a new way to the stew. Allow me to make a pronouncement that I have not made for a very long time: I am divine. I know this right down my spine and into my shoes. I do not have the blues any more and underscoring this and that for attention is not my intention. The core of my being accepts this as fulfillment.

The more I am has opened the door to ever-more and the basis of understanding here and now came into me as a WOW!, that I had not expected, and so I found it quite hard to accept, except as a hardship. I felt so shook up and irretrievable, it was unbelievable. As I look at it all now, in hindsight, I can take a second look at it with kinder eyes and without the surprise factor, it seems quite clear. Angels held me near.

Let me tell you a story:

A prisoner once found a watch in the corner of his cell. It was an old, worn timepiece from the passed. So he asked, "Who does this watch belong to?"

A voice from *the passed* answered, "I am the beauty of time, surpassed. All is everlasting, you know. I came to show you that, with this watch. This watch is the watch of the watcher, based solely on time's passing, and it has no depth of substantiation. For, time is of the essence and essence speaks of depth-perception way beyond time. Keep this timepiece as a memento, but remember its voice from *the passed* speaking out loud.

"All is allowed in time's timelessness. That is the depth perception of this timeless moment, that speaks of all that has passed and so much more to come.

"Beat the drum of that, to understand the absolute beauty of time's timeless way to say: All is well, now and forever.

"Everything created in time is."

Timelessness in Time

Life is a river and all is in it.

All can look upstream and curse the darkness of pinched-off perspective, but this is not a requirement of all-orchestrated living.

Love is a deep, heartfelt decision. I make a decision to love the depth of life I am, as a star of all that is shining, here and now perfection.

I elect all to the office of absolute universal-authorship. Universal heart-authority is according to the unique streaming of the heartfelt dream of all I am. I bar none from the portal of peace I am. I naturally am freedom's door to evermore. Everlasting love effortlessly presents, as the gift of life it is, to, through and around all as the countenance of now I am, unfolding the all-spacious universal heart's song, singing itself within the eternal grace note of now, creating a softer view of the wholesome stew all reside in.

The strand at my command, I solidly am here and now on purpose.

Human bondage or golden strand, I decide
Stranded or absolutely connected, I decide
Lonely or never alone, I decide
Practiced or principled, I decide
Looking on or insightful, I decide
A hole or a whole, I decide
Beginning and ending or continuum, I decide
Lackluster or shining, I decide
Instrument or instrumental, I decide
Static or steady flow, I decide
Upstream or downstream, I decide
Orphaned or soul-sponsored, I decide
Warring or peaceful, I decide

Wary or trusting, I decide
Armed or disarming, I decide
Pleasing or pleasant, I decide
Aloof or warm-hearted, I decide
Dull or crystal clear, I decide
Revered or reverential, I decide
Artifact or deliberate creation, I decide
Struggle or joyful co-creating, I decide
Personal or persona non grata, I decide
Heroic or being, I decide.

All

I am the message
I am the message center
I am the giver
I am the receiver
I am the white
I am the black
I am the rainbow
I am the rain
I am the dreamer
I am the dream
I am the reluctance
I am the freedom within
I am the spade
I am the dirt
I am the chorus
I am the song
I am all
I am nothing at all
I am peace
I am war
I am all that is, every view
I am Source, all in me and you
Together we travel
Together we twine
Together we're freedom
Ripe on the vine.

Soul-Essence

I n the garden, on the north side of the mountain, there was a river of pure gold. Waiting for water, the mouse never saw the gold, but hurried from place to place, looking for water for the flowers she tended.

The gold flowed freely and lit up the darkness of the north face of the mountain. Still the mouse searched and wearied herself to such an extent that she fell amid the flowers she tended and they spoke to her of love alone.

"Fear not, mouse. The river of gold contains goodness for all. Be still and receive the river's blessings." The mouse had no choice. She was exhausted and lay still and accepted the beauty of the river's gold.

Just then, a mountain lion came by to drink at the river's edge. Seeing the golden river, he said, "This river has been good for the flowers and good for the mouse. It must be good for me." He drank deeply at this place. Soon, he lay happily by the mouse, purring and licking his paws. "What have we to fear?" he asked. "We are all well provided for—not in the way we had imagined, and yet far beyond our minds' imaginings. We are fulfilled and satisfied by a river of pure gold."

More and more life appeared at the river, and all grew from the experience, until one day a boy wandered by with a fishing line and found his feet in the river. The blessings of the river grew within him, and soon his fishing bucket was full of fish. He doubted the river's nourishments and so refused to see the beauty there. His line was suddenly sitting in water, and no fish appeared for his lunch. "I must have been dreaming!" he said.

Building Blocks of Belief

Beneath the transparent cloak of a source understanding, there is absolute acceptance and allowing of an ever-present knowing or universal wisdom, from within, to naturally be a part of all life.

We sometimes worry about what it is we have to offer or share with others. We may agonize about our purpose here in this space of time. The simplicity of the answer to this question may make you smile. What our purpose is or what we have to offer or share in any existence is our *life-flow*. That is all there is.

The rest is a jumble of the mind's creation, for us to view more softly, to see the illusion with joy and enjoy all of it as an experience. Our capability to see our vibrational flow as endless creative possibilities comes when our life is seen, from within, as boundless potential moving through to *choose* from. Let it be your unique experience.

Ever Bright Wind Walker

Hold the chorus of the song
So others hear and sing along
Imagine Grace is in your hand
An easy friend at your command

Admit the trials that set you free
And settle to the truth you see
The inner shutter, open wide
Reveals the more of you inside

All windswept reaches now have sun
The inner child is filled with fun
The spinner's web is set to flow
With warp and weft of all who know

And still the silent forces grin
So happy to see you again
Alive and filled with all who love
With every view from up above

Enter the magic, the lightening dance
Whipped up from nothing in a flash
Connection of dreamers and spinners of tales
Of lions, elephants and spouting whales

Right from the heart and let her rip
As from the kindness cup you sip
The circle of life goes on and on
The door is open, the lights are on.

Horse Power

Nowness found you yesterday
And wrote to you a song
If you listen openly
You'll start to hum along

It isn't loud and boisterous
It's subtle, soft and clear
It is the song of freedom
It is the song so near

Your feathers are arriving
They're almost into view
You'll feel them in your lightness
With everything you do

The sands of time that grate you
Are washing from your heart
And in their place a vision
Begins a brand-new start

So face your horse into the wind
And watch its mane unfurl
There is no foe to conquer
There never was a whirl

You are the blessed blessing
And all you do is love
Your armaments are lifting
To free the snow white dove

Remain the mantra's message

Of peace in every cell
Collide with truth and sense love
No heaven and no hell

Bright star on the horizon
Drop down into the sea
Let your arc carve with ashes
The all that's meant to be

We are the Trojan's whisper
We are the silent hoof
All care, all light, all loving
All dancing on the roof

Today is just a vista
For us to see the light
And open, without asking
To sing with all our might

So know you are the lover
The war within is done
Stand tall with all securely
And radiate the sun.

The Dragon Speaks

The dragon speaks of many things
Of circuses and all their rings
A soul survivor does declare
I see these dragons everywhere

Their feet are funny, festive, too
Their teeth surround the thing they do
Blossoming is their deed most fair
You'll find their flowers in their lair

They speak of lions, tigers, kings
They speak of circles, rivers, rings
There's mist surrounding lives they lead
It's soft and fuzzy, please take heed

The dragon is a kindly soul
And slaying folk is not his goal
A shrewd conceiver of the flame
He knows that we are all one name

So let the dragon in you bloom
See all the light and not the gloom
Balloons of magic raise you high
To see into the dragon's eye

Reflections of your own sweet truth
A heart so pure, a glistening tooth
And oh, the flame of this true one
Alive and well and in the sun

So give your dragon-self a break
And see the truth in all you spake
The legend of the dragon lives
In life he breathes and love he gives.

How Soft is Love?

Once upon a time, when elves were tall and fairies small and the balance of the forest was understood by all, there lived a tall elf named Lulu. Lulu wasn't her *heart name*, so she called herself Love Eyes. The forest folk absolutely understood the name Love Eyes and so they named their tall elf friend Lulu Love Eyes, for Lulu saw everything through the eyes of love alone.

One day, deep in the heart of the forest, a small child arrived. This child was so beautiful, no one cared at all if it was a boy or a girl, if it had red hair or black hair or no hair at all. The forest folk loved this child. They wanted Lulu Love Eyes to see this child, too. They sent a message with a tiny fairy to bring Lulu to the heart of the forest. On a day when sharing and caring and being part of all that is was in the air, Lulu Love Eyes saw beauty at the heart of the forest, for this is what the forest folk named the small child.

Lulu knew the truth of beauty immediately. She smiled one of those deep, knowing smiles that make your heart sing. She asked the forest folk a question to make them understand the arrival of this beautiful child. The question was this: "How soft is Love?"

"Well, that's a weird question," a gnome said. "Is Love soft?"

"Let me see," said the tiger. "I feel soft after I eat a gazelle and I love gazelle."

"Oh, for heaven's sake," said an antelope. "What does this really mean?"

Lulu Love Eyes began to explain.

"This child is the beauty of all of you, together. In your soft view of this child, you have created a miracle called life in the forest. This child is a reminder of who you truly are. You are love. When you look at this child, you forget all else. Your heart melts and you would do anything for each other. You share your love with each other in looking at this child, for you remember the softness of love.

"Love has no hard bits or pokey corners. It has no stiffness or refusing to be. It has no coldness or icy stares. Love is radiantly soft. It is mist and fluffiness. It is fluid and swish. It is beckoning forward and open arms."

The zebra, who was a balance of black and white, could see love's softness in his fur. The crocodile could sense love's softness in his smile. The leopard could flow with love's softness in his intricate pattern. The wallaby could boing with love's softness in his bounce. The willow could feel love's softness in her weeping branches. The watermelon could hold love's softness in her seeds. The orange could taste love's softness in her juice. The whale, who came all the way into the heart of the forest from the ocean to see beauty, could blow love's softness in his spout. Each form of life in the forest shared in expressing the softness of love they uniquely experienced.

Lulu Love Eyes, seeing the harmony and balance of all expressions in the forest, said,

"Let us never forget the softness of love. Then the forest will always be our home."

New Understanding

Hang on to that new kite
No, just let it go
The answer to holding
Is just let it flow

No fancy maneuvers
No quick-witted strides
To stay in this soft flow
Will let go of pride

Our vision of union
Is safe in our heart
Let go of truth's concept
And just play your part

Remember the dragon
His flame and his spark?
In his true expression
He lights up the dark

Telepathy calls you
Now answer the call
Within your connection
You'll be love to all.

Self-Acceptance

Dear Love:
   Please assist me to love my subtle defenses enough to invite them, with open arms, into the light of being, so they may see clearly that there are no fences in truth. Please assist my heart to sense the humour in this illusory tactic of invitation into now, for now is all there ever is, was or will be.

The head becomes serious at this notion of residential self-inclusion. The heart says, Yes, this place of absolute acceptance is something I remember like an old, trusted, friend. Come and be one with life, love. Flow with all hearts and see the sun all is in your shining. Breast your cards no longer. Lay them fully out on the table to fit with the hands of all.

Together we will play a new game, and the winner doesn't take all. It is all. *United we stand and divided we fall* is magic in the place of inner knowing.

Lightbeams, unite. It is time to grow in the same direction—up! Your flashlight will never need batteries again, and it will shine in all directions. Power failures will be up to the individual soul's choosing love and directly dialing in. Source is the endless supply of love.

Please assist my heart to remain open and free, love, to see how to be. Self-abandonment is not who I am. The love I am simply is. My heart has caught the wave. Salute!

Unique Connection

Fluid and free, the mighty oak sows the seeds of truth it is born to plant. It does not question its existence, conditions or the seed it bears. This unique expression stands where it is planted and becomes stronger and stronger with all life surrounding it. The oak's physical aspect is not its strength. The life that flows through and around it is.

The support and interconnection of the life surrounding the oak assist it to be its unique expression. The pine next to the oak does not expect the oak to produce pine needles or pine cones, and the grass at its feet does not expect the oak to sprout blades of grass. The oak is the vibration it needs to be to do what it intended to do as an oak seed.

Within the seeds of the oak, all of its inherent strength and beauty exist and the same is true of all life. Expectations do not change the truth of your seed. Thrive in natural connection to all life, not knowing the depth of what these may uniquely be. Know that everything required, not unlike the oak, is within easy reach, from within you. Life comes through your core from the roots of all existence. Even in the toughest of conditions, your eternal core is strong. Turn to your core and stand strong in your nature of absolute connection with life. Feel free in this.

Weasel Love

On a cold sunny morning in late July, a weasel named McGarrion strolled down his favourite avenue in search of love. Now, weasels are no strangers to the art of making love. They are indeed love personified with their enticing weasel grins, weaselly eyes and sporty weasel whiskers. McGarrion had come of age, so to speak, and his little heart was wide open for the wiles of a woman weasel. He wandered to and fro in the thicket and crossed Main Street a half dozen times before he caught the scent of a woman. Following his nose was not new for weasels, either. They have been in the know since attraction of the species came into vogue and Adam himself could enlighten you on that topic.

Back at the thicket, McGarrion had zeroed in on a hip chick named Rosie. According to divine plan, McGarrion went right for the coupling, but Rosie had other ideas. Was this the weasel of her dreams? Would he nurture and provide for her and her progeny? Did he set her heart on fire? It was all about smell for McGarrion, but for Rosie, there was a lot of discerning to do, and she stood back and watched while McGarrion displayed his manly charms to feel that feeling deep within that this is the one, the one to unite with and create a home for something more. For days these two young weasels danced through the woods playing hide and seek, displaying and discerning until one fine Friday at five o'clock, Rosie felt certain of McGarrion's sincerity and steadfast pursuit of her charms.

Honesty didn't play a part in this play, for there was nothing dishonest in any part of this pursuit but truth was ever-present. The scene and selection of subject matter were never discussed. They just occurred. A gentle occurrence, deep in the forest, found McGarrion and Rosie busy and connected for some time. Then at just the right time and not a minute before, these two would proudly present their offspring to the forest floor without discussion or preamble. Timing was important, and so a subtle sense known only to the weasel and source came into play, and tonight the thicket knew the reason behind all of the rumbling and squeaking inside this hole on Forth-right Street. Mama Rosie and Papa McGarrion paraded their young cautiously out to inspect their training grounds, where, for the next long while, lessons big and small would be learned.

A handsomer family could not have been found. The love and the light could be felt all around. The girl of his dreams and the man she had found were now one.

I Know This Elf

I know this elf
I know him well
I know he has
A tale to tell

I see his feet
I sense his hand
I know he moves
At his command

Into the ice
I see him go
Into the sleet
Into the snow

With his true heart
I feel the beat
I feel the love
I feel the heat

I know the logic
Of his mind
I know he leaves
All doubt behind

I see him standing
Once again
Inside the forest
Of the glen

Oh, merry elf
I know your worth
I wish you well
I wish you mirth

I wish you rainbows
Every day
I wish you sun
I wish you play

The setting sun
Will see you born
Into a day
That starts at morn

And you will know
Within your birth
The lessons learned
Were not a curse

Oh, curious elf
Let go my hand
For you will move
At love's command

The to and fro
Of yesterday
Will be the know
Of every day

I wish you whole

I set you free
Within my soul
I let you be.

Universal Heart of All

Beggars can't be choosers, it is said, and yet they are.
The body follows every star that's born within your heart.

Make a choice, decide today
To help yourself to find a way
To mentor every child you see
To aid the light to let it be

A crucifixion is just a storm
Within a heart that's never torn
The bread of life is always free
The fruit you bear is from *that* tree

A constable of noble blood
Cannot control a holy flood
Or end the tears of Evermore
Arriving now to cleanse the floor

A fixing, fasting, racist ride
Is not the thing to change the tide
A softly swelling poem of truth
Is moving now to raise the roof

Pigeons take the message true
That love springs full in all you do
A balance truer than the sword
Where love shines through without a word

A cleanly shaven head will shine

On everything that is divine
A non-divided heart will see
The all is well and let it be.

Bona Fide Traveler

Issues of abuse fade and die
Hungry for the light, faith arrives
Fleeing nothing, you stay
And in the light is revealed
The more you are

Complete and whole, you face the music
And dance to a new tune
It is the song of life that has
Always played in the background
Now you recognize this old tune
And you love it—every chorus

In living, you forget dying
And an old friend slips away
A requiem of peace and solitude
Awakes a spark of life, long forgotten
Footsteps lead to an old well
Where truth is waiting

Hands across the waters
Hands across the seas
Hands forever serving
All the love that is

Sarcasm resides in the parting of ways
Protective views not needed
Every office of the truth is here to stay
Surrender to the knowing
Soon you will be glowing.

Patterns

Old patterns hold us until we show them the love that is this endless day of peace and quietude. Joy awaits the opening bud. The pain will increase, but the reality of this pain will be known by you. Keep to the hearth and warmth will surround you and steady your view. You are the keeper of your own soul—maintain it well.

The spires of a greater Church ring a bell for absolute freedom, and your ears hear the peal of this bell and answer the call you now know to be for you and all. Chapter one begins with a blessing to all and a description of abundance not yet known. The words will come to you and you will have the understanding to go with them. Trust your open heart to be the fountain of faith you are—forever true, within.

Spiders are gathering in every size and pattern of joy to share the weaving of a new matrix to hold the truth more securely and begin the building of a new foundation of belief that will encompass the now, unfolding. Forever-true will behold the groundswell of gratitude rising to cleanse the view of all. Hold onto your hat or better still, let your hat go where it needs to go, without holding.

Funerals will come, some in physical form and some in death of an old view held. Welcome them all, standing firmly yet flexibly, in the *all is well*, whispering your name and knowing your signature is none other than love-alone.

The keeper of the keys is always you. The holder of the train, the scepter and the mantle is, as well. For you are all things and all things are you. A paradox for certain, but then truth is filled with paradox in this world-view. Are the kindly kind? Are the sisters sisterly? Are the knights knightly?

When the truth prevails, the paradox vanishes and clarity arises, naturally.

Acclimatation

It was dawn and a group gathered in the garden by a rock wall that was crumbling, next to the church.

The hammer that broke this wall was not visible and yet it was as forceful as any visible hammer. It was a tide. Not the usual tide. It was an even tide. It was a place of absolute peace, a still point of the open heart. It was a song on the wind. It was a passion rising.

The group gathering was aware of the force of this hammer. It held understanding of the past and hope for a speedy recovery through planting seeds of hope in the true wind with helping hands and waiting patiently until acclimatation felled the wall of ignorance and let the great light shine once more on the only Church that mattered: *The Great Sisterhood of all.*

Simple Freedom

I know the love of all that flows
Is not a bitter pill
In lifting up the veil to see
And settling the will

A kinder view of all that is
Arrives with daily bread
I'm seeing from a new space now
The heart and not the head

The judging of myself I knew
Is coming into view
And so I see the pain I wrought
Was never about you

King and kinship in the air
All lightness and a flow
True beauty in all glows, I see
With everything I know

Today the compass knows the way
And no waves do I see
Clear sailing on the sea of life
When I just *let it be.*

Take it Easy

"Bother, bother," said the muskrat as he rushed to set his affairs in order and undo the mess he had created in the sleepy hollow. "It isn't working out as I had planned and—oh!—my head is spinning. I must do this and this and I must be done before nine o'clock. How can I do this? My friends are expecting tea at nine o'clock and everything has gone awry!"

"Slow down," said the toad. "Nothing in this world is important enough to make yourself sick over, my friend. Here, have a chair. Take a load off. Sit awhile with me and you will see things much more clearly."

"Do you think so?" asked the muskrat.

"*I know so,*" said the toad. "Do you remember when this hollow had lush green valleys and meadowlarks and every type of flower bloomed along the path?"

"Oh, that was a while ago," said the muskrat. "I forgot about that."

The toad continued, "The settlers moved into the valley and began their busyness and nothing has been still since. I miss those days."

"Me, too," said the muskrat. "Never mind the tidying. Let's sit and smell the honey and biscuits until our guests arrive, and we will rest and remember the quiet goodness."

"Sounds good to me," said the toad.

And so it was that deep in the ground, beneath the roots of an old, old cherry tree, a muskrat and a toad reunited in deep remembering of their connection to what served their soul.

Solace

Around the bend and in the hive
Where all the bees are so alive
There is a jumble and a rhyme
Far beyond all space and time

And if you listen close, you'll see
The crossroads of the you in me
No matter what the road you take
The me in you, you cannot shake

For we are bound with all at sea
And through this rope, we all will be
Beneath the roots of this great one
The all-eternal midnight sun.

The Point

"What is the point?" the man asked. "Here I am, on this road to God knows where, with this donkey that will not listen!"

Another man on the road beside him stopped and put his hand on the first man's shoulder. He smiled the smile of understanding and compassion. "It does seem futile at times, doesn't it?" he asked. "The point is, What *is* the point? The point of clarity is just being on this road together and knowing that beyond the will of this donkey that we all lead, this road is never God-forsaken.

"When we look down, we see the donkey, its load, its sweat and its mule-like nature, which we are not accepting of in ourselves. We see our base metal and it looks tarnished on this road. When we look up, we remember the sun that never leaves us and its warmth and comfort. We close our eyes from the brightness and feel the relaxation of the sun's rays, which fully fill us. We stop a spell to absorb this warmth and our donkey gets a rest.

"I never thought of it that way!" said the first man. "I can feel what you are saying."

The donkey brayed loudly in agreement.

"Oh, it isn't in the thinking," the second man said. "It is in the feeling. It is always in the feeling. Feel your life as you expressed it to me. Life on this road is to be experienced fully and in the feeling—you know the point. You always do. Let your load rest and feel the lightness. That is the point."

The Heart of Man

Lead me, Lord, to the heart of man
No surface rights, no bones to scan
A clear reflection of all life
To know the truth and without strife

A beacon beckons, a song is heard
A whisper from a spirit-bird
All holy, hallowed in silent prayer
Resolves a frenzy in the air

And so the melting pot is seen
No holy water and no obscene
And on the altar beside the tide
A place to pause and bless this ride

A rhythm of a glacial glance
A pulse of life's awakened dance
A freely flying, unfolding flow
Foundational to the all we know

Expend the energy, feel the boost
Live the moment of love-let-loose
Create the life you wish to live
Receiving fully to fully give

Alabaster and crimson red
Blessings on the holy bed
A transportation of new supplies
Devoid of fear or lack or lies.

Endless Abundance

A long time ago on the Isle of Crete there lived a baker whose bread was so popular, people came from every direction to buy it for their meals. The texture of the bread was so fine. The lightness of the bread was amazing. The taste of this bread stayed with you the whole day through, and its memory lingered on in your mind. This baker was up early and to bed late. The demand for his bread was so high that his business thrived and his coffers filled with money. In the evening, he would say a prayer of thanks for the lightness and taste of his loaves and for his thriving business that fed and kept him and his family so well.

Then one summer there was a terrible draught and there was no flour to speak of to make bread. The baker bought whatever oats he could buy, but they were soon depleted and his supply of bread dwindled, as well. He had to dip into his savings to feed and clothe himself and his family, and he began to wonder where his next source of funding would come from. He had never done any other job in his lifetime. He had always been a baker like his own father and his grandfather before him. He had so much time on his hands now, and in this time he thought and thought about what he would do in place of baking.

One summer morning in early May, a peddler came to his door and asked, "May I borrow your ladder to get my cat down out of that tall tree beyond the firehouse?"

"Of course," said the baker. "Let me help you with it. It is very heavy."

The two men sported the ladder on their shoulders and marched it over to the tree where the cat was hiding. The mission of the peddler was to fetch his runaway cat and be on his way, until he heard of the town's dilemma.

"No grain?" he asked. "What a plight. I will stay and feed you, for making meals from nothing is my specialty. I am a diviner of soul

food. This is the food that fills you up like no other food ever can."
The baker had never heard of such a thing, but he was desperate and
ready to try something new. He asked the peddler to carry on.

The peddler centered himself and began to sing the most beautiful music. The music drifted across the townspeople and it was so
enjoyable, their eyes were filled with tears of joy. Then the peddler
spread vibrant colours across the land. The crops began to flesh out
as the soil began to moisten and reclaim itself from the townsfolks'
tears. The cornfield sprouted new stocks and the fishing hole filled
with blue-green water full of fish. The peddler kept on singing and
spreading colour until the valley was restored to its natural grace
and ease. The peddler saw that his job was done in the valley, and he
packed his bags, secured his cat and moved on.

The baker began to bake again as soon as the wheat field ripened
and the harvest was brought in. He never forgot the magic of this
unexpected visitor to his town. He felt the wonder of this restora-
tion until the day he died. He remembered the joyful music and the
colourful flow that brought tears of pure joy to restore the natural
balance of his existence here in his homeland on the Isle of Crete. He
was never hungry again.

Peace of the Heart

A group of marching soldiers stopped for a break on the hot, dusty road. They found a cool spot in the shade by a riverbank and began to share their hearts with each other.

"Are we marching to war to take all that is unclaimed before others take it?" asked one.

"No, we are marching to war to take all that was always ours and others have taken it away from us," said another.

"Well, that's not what I've been told," said a third. "My father and grandfather were always soldiers and so am I. I am marching to war to hold up our family tradition of being warriors."

A young man of nineteen, hearing all of these comments, found them quite enlightening. He thanked the soldiers for their remarks. He said, "Deep in your hearts is the same love that is deep in mine. This love is never depleted. It is always there when we see love. These old views of war do not fit any longer. They do not make any sense to my heart. You are my brother as I am yours. If the *military* had taught you about universal love, would you believe it? If you had been taught of the endless supply of love from your open heart when you were a child, would you even be here now? If your family had held love above war, would you see this marching to war with softer eyes? Look to the source of your beliefs and question them. Is it truly your heart's desire to march to war?"

"Well, then, why are you here?" asked the first soldier of this young man.

"I am weary of fighting the war within." said the young man. "I decided to join you here to see and feel what war was really all about. I see that you are all as misguided as I. Now I finally see that my heart was my touchstone from the start. I will go home and remember that the fruits of war are more war, while the fruits of the heart are love-alone. Today, you have given me a gift of the highest order. It is a medal of bravery to fight for the right to be free in my heart.

To do this, I will remain true to my heart-understanding and be very still to remember my commitment to the beauty of the infinite heart-connection of all.

"Thank you all. I now know that my view is the battlefield, and love-alone wins every battle hands down. If your heart is not in it, you cannot win. The prize is always the same as the objective. Consider your objective. What is it you want? Is it love or war? The answers you receive will always be as beautiful as the questions you ask."

Puzzles

In the light of a new day, four crossword puzzles decided to solve themselves. They crossed the lines out from within themselves and set new parameters for their very definition. One puzzle said, "The script that is written is not the truth of who I am. There is a larger puzzle to consider here, and it is every thought upon every other unto eternity."

"What do you mean?" asked the second puzzle. "I don't understand the scope of what you are saying."

"I get it," said the third puzzle "There is no puzzle at all! There is just a remembering of truth. I feel what you say in my heart."

The fourth puzzle thought the other three had all gone completely mad and started to recreate the lines within his puzzle frame. He felt fearful and confused. He felt lost in the matrix of his mind and, for just a moment, he forgot the love he was.

Then he looked at the other three puzzles sharing their hearts and encouraging him to do the same, and he melted. His puzzle lines became wobbly and limp and fell off again. In the stillness of this space, he felt his freedom so intensely, he began to sing and dance. He felt the joy he was, deep within his heart, and he knew the old puzzle lines he had held, to dare anyone to figure him out, were quite funny. He laughed softly within and felt a compassionate view of himself and thus, of all.

The four puzzles joined hands and their outside, thick lines disappeared, as well. They felt the one heart they were, together, and they no longer had to figure anything out. They could just be free and let all be.

Vibrational Being

Questions and answers, questions and answers, and the answer always comes back to love, for love is the answer to all questioning.

Let us begin. A long time ago, when the earth was thought to be flat, a fat cat spoke to a passing mouse of the grace of the whole human race. "Be well, mouse, no matter what is going on in your living. For all is uneventfully well, and the eventide of all wellness presents at the crossroads of every intersection in your life. There you will intrinsically know to turn left, right, up or down, according to your own true heart's knowing way.

"Spacious though your heart may seem, it is eternally and unlimitedly expanding itself to include all, even as all expands to include all that has become and all that is ever becoming. How do I know this, you ask? I just do, beyond any reasoning or thought-processing and beyond any words or self-mockery."

"I know, deep within my heart of all hearts, what I know and this is a deep resonating knowing that has served me so well throughout all of my lives lived.

"I do not doubt my knowing any longer. I am stronger in self-trust than ever before, and so much more self-trust is becoming, I will know myself *off by heart* very soon. Then, the spoon of all spoons I am will begin to feed soul food naturally to all."

Love's Wisdom in All

"See this light?" asked the mongoose. "It is the light of love and truth. Trust is its objective of all objectives and it knows full well how to move itself to full trust within truth."

"Forsooth?" asked the weasel. "Is this about forsooth?"

"Forsooth is in the tooth," said the mongoose. "It is in the natural wisdom held, that forsooth is naturally born in us all and passed on to others beyond reason, belief or spoken word. The wisdom of forsooth is lovingly shared by the natural wisdom of the opened heart."

"Can I play my part?" asked the butterfly.

"Of course you can!" replied the Wisdom of All. "It is your call and we hear you calling again just like you always did when awareness filled the valley and the mountaintops rang with the resonance of eternal strength for all to hear with the ears of love from above the din of all noise."

The mountain lion woke and looked down into the valley of kings. He knew his place in the kingdom again, and he began to purr a low purr that resonated right through the whole mountain and down into the valley floor. It became more and more resonant, and it soothed the hearts of all fear-filled beings, settling them to slumber. This vibration became one with the golden ring of eternal love which joined itself obsequiously, without another thought.

Love was bought and no money changed hands, but a wide open purse presented itself to the universal flow, and everyone could know what dreams are made of and the endless wealth from which they all eternally flow, glow and go in unending circles as life.

Bunnies of peace joined the circle in leaps and bounds and a gentle, soft circling began all over again.

The Sailor and His Crew

There was a sailor who sailed the high seas of life. He had a long-standing crew and he knew them so well. He knew their soul-song like the back of his hand and so much more. If his crew was *up*, the sailor picked up on it and rejoiced with his face into the wind and his hair straight back in the glory of the winds of change. He rode the waving of his own heart's desire. When his crew was *down*, this sailor sat with them. He never left their side in spirit. He was always there for them and the crew knew this so deeply. It assisted them all to ride the seas of life in endless ways and to know their back was covered by the captain of their ship.

The sailor and his crew sailed into the Doldrums one day, just as the sun was setting. They sat in the windless sea and waited and waited and waited and guess what? No winds of change blew! This was so unusual. It felt oddly debilitating. The sailor and his crew were so used to the height of the high-waving experiences, they could not even conceive of stillness and calm Sargasso seas. They did not at first see this as just another type of experience. They started to look at each other with deep perplexing tones, moans and groans and say, "Oh, no! Now what? How will we do this? Is this possible? Can we withstand this as captain and crew?"

After much shifting and shaking and low belly-aching, this captain and crew accepted what presented, and in the absolute acceptance of silent stillness and uncomplicated being, the winds of change, taking them all to a new part of the ocean of endless waving possibilities and all else, began to blow. They all saw, as one huge *aha*, how they could best assist each other in any situational presentation, with how to just be with life fully and to accept it completely—wholeheartedly.

In the highest waves and in the lowest troughs, in the moonlit glints and sudden thaws, this captain and crew found their whole-ness presentation as one beauty-filled united family for all to see, to know and to understand that all is essentially, everlastingly well. They all could tell from within. They began again as a dream team of nine to align with the sign that brought them all together as one sailing force and of course a new crew member presented itself as a beautiful elf of exceptional kindness and became all it could become from the example of the Nine that were so divinely guided.

Inroads of Love

ove will find a way. Trust Love. Love comes into life in unlimited fashions that will blow your mind sky-high.

There once was a man who was pushing through roads into new frontiers. He was surveying his *clearings* one evening and looking at a new roadway he was opening up into the core of the frontier, up north. It was spring. The snow and ice had gone, but the ground was still cold and wet. As he walked this new road that he had worked so hard on, to give all access to the core of this new frontier, he saw clearly that there was a huge flat-deck truck crossways on his road, blocking the whole road off. He stopped to observe this presentation upon his path to progressive-clearing into new frontiers and into the core or heart of the north. At first, he thought his way was solidly blocked.

He almost gave up even considering this particular inroad. Then in a brilliant flash of deep insightfulness, he knew that the love of Source was already *on* the other side of this flat-deck, and so he was unstoppable because he is love and love is everywhere—everywhere! He just knew this truth as a felt sense. He did not think it. He did not believe it. It was not a hope or faith that he carried inside. He knew as a deep knower of wisdom knows. He knew from the depth of his knowing heart that love is everywhere and that the Source he is had imagined the endless possibilities of this breakthrough road into the core of the frozen north—the core of every frozen emotional holding anyone could conceptualize.

The universal heart's desire for more fluidity, warmth and caring went ahead of this man and naturally manifested, beyond words or beliefs, a unique way for Source, as the love that animates all, to continue right on of its own unstoppable accord to manifest this road of all roads into the heart of the Great White North, so the rivers of love could flow once again and warmth would once more return to the north.

It was a north-meets-south kind of dream. It was a crown-meets-root conveyance and, in the heart of it all, love did what love always does. Love loved its way where it intrinsically knew how to love, and inroads built themselves right past any obstacles presenting in a physical focus. For obstacles create a desire for more, and more presents itself in unlimited ways as more loving consciousness, just as soon as allowing occurs. In the fine art of absolute allowing, this is called *love, beyond measure.*

The Bat

Behind a waterfall there lived a bat. Now, bats are considered to be blind, but this bat had such amazing inner eyes and echo-location systems, he could sense teensy, tiny insects that might have *bugged* others but were just a delicious meal for him. He gathered them all up and filled his cup to overflowing, knowing that irritants held no power over him.

Now, no matter the weather, this fully sighted bat knows where to go, do and be all that he is and to see beyond a worldly view that all is in perfect order behind the emotional curtain presenting in this physical focus.

He flies here and there without a care in the world, caring for himself so he can care for all in being fully fed himself. It took him only a short while to intuit this was so, and now he knows, deep within his ears so clear, that love is very, very near at all times.

The bend in the road taught bat so much. It was his crutch to support him to see and to be creation's wholeness-presentation, approving of itself 100% and *heaven-sent* to boot. The crutch was the offshoot of: *I spy with my little eye, something that is red*. Then it was his compunction for going on ahead and grounding to the heart of all hearts to fully play the part of parts that is only his to play on this fine day of all days. He put the emphasis on the *play*. It makes it all easier, and ease is what life is all about. He shouts, "I'm alive and living the love of life!"

A warthog of light popped in to say, "Hey, there is no sin in the *where have you been*? Catching up to yourself is the stuff that dreams are made of. Just when you think you've got it, the whole play rearranges, and changes occur that propel you in another direction. Direct yourself in the ease and grace of all living free to be and see the difference all around you.

"There'll be some changes made.

"Lie back and enjoy the changes. Put your feet up. You deserve a break. Take it, lickety- split, allowing it all to fit with your heart—the smartest part of the play you play with all.

"It's your call!"

Bird of Love

On a windswept terrace, a young bird sat waiting for its mother to return. It had fallen from its nest and was resting for awhile, trying hard to smile as only a bird of beauty can. She shivered and fluffed out her feathers, insulating her small body from the winds of change buffeting her now. As she sat and looked about herself, her eyes were wide with expectation. She had never been flat on the ground before, and it scared her a little. It was a new view of the stew she resided in, and she felt a little exposed in the openness of this large, windswept space.

A dog of peace came by with a soulful eye and put his nose up to her, saying, "Be still beautiful bird. Your mother knows you fully wherever you are. The mothering instinct is so strong. She will find you and feed you soul food. She will teach you how to fly beyond belief of flying. You will see the natural process of it all. You see, you haven't fallen at all. You are just seeing and learning from a new vantage point. Be open to the lesson, bird of love. Be open to the beauty of the beast you are, with new eyes. The eyes of love you are, allow you to see far beyond this place in time. So realign your eye to inner sight and, looking deeply, you will see beyond self-fighting. Believe in yourself, bird, in the wordless resonance of being you are, with all in this hall of transformation.

"The nation of the one sun warmly shines on your head and dread leaves you. Then you begin to explore the possibilities of closer inspection of this section of the *decked perspective* to find the beauty there and everywhere. This is an eye-opener. As comfort arrives, your mother dives down to feed and comfort you and you share with her your journey of the mind. She reminds you of your journey of the heart. There, you see a new part you can play in the art of making love, and you willingly begin, past the din of the mind, reminding yourself of what your mother said.

"Gently, softly and surely you see your way day to day, from within your ever-smart heart ,and you see your part more comprehensively and change gears to be nearer to yourself.

"You may not see what I see," said the dog of light, "for I see the love you are and I know your deep capability from within, past the din of your mind. I have always seen in this way. This is my intrinsic nature. I love your heart-song beyond words, dear bird of love!"

Know the wellness you already are from within. Study your inner landscape by being in it and by surveying the wholeness it is with all.

Joyful Connection

The swim instructor sat by the edge of the pool. She directed from an exterior view and the lessons passed one week at a time. Her so-called students were not catching on to the style of this instructor because she wasn't expressing herself as she felt herself to be—fully in herself and expressing the fullness of her unique expression for all to synthesize.

Then a young swimmer said, "I'm having trouble floating."

This woke the swim instructor up. She didn't pre-think this would wake her up, but on some level or layer of her being, she pre-cognized it would wake her up, and it did! She was such a natural swimmer, she couldn't even fathom a child not knowing how to float easily. The swim instructor paid close attention to this child speaking out about its difficulty and asking for assistance. She went within herself and looked back, way back, on her life of swimming from its inception. What was the key to her natural floating capability? She mused, and after a short time she realized it was her deep love of the *feeling* of floating. Floating in water allowed her to feel free as a bird in flight. She felt passionate about feeling this feeling—the up and down of it, the back and forth of it and the free flow of it. She felt so uninhibited floating in water that she could just deeply relax and enjoy the moment easily, as a felt-sense of pure joyful freedom to go with the flow of her intended movement.

The swim lesson ended, and the youthful swim instructor took the child having difficulty aside. She was drawn to say to the child, "Do you have a fear of drowning?"

The child did not hesitate. She said, "Yes, I do!"

The instructor didn't need to know the story behind this fear. She asked the child if she was willing to let go of her fear.

"Yes," said the child.

"Great!" said the instructor. "Let us begin to feel the freedom of floating."

The two of them worked together in close connection, co-creating a way that would allow the child to willingly float and flow without feeling fear. With each step, the instructor and the child learned a new way to share themselves in co-operation with one another without resistance, but as pleased them both deeply. The instructor learned to deeply share her feelings verbally and the student learned to listen to the instructor's natural passion for floating. This passionate expression of deep joy excited the child's heart to try and try and try again as she felt able.

The child could be any child. The instructor could be any instructor. The situation could be any situation. The co-creation could be any co-creation. The passion could be any passion. The fear could be any fear. The bottom line is that there is a way to connect beyond fear and complacency. This way presents itself in wondrously diverse ways. This way is love.

Quintessence

The quintessential essence
Of a quintessential ghost
Is the clockwork in the window
Of the one you love the most

Though the chime will never tell you
And the time is standing still
Still the essence of the clockwork
Is reflected on the sill

As the hue beyond the window
Turns a misty shade of gray
All the language of the shadow
Loses all it has to say

Let the warmth of every windscreen
Turn its shadow from the cold
And relax within the knowing
Of the all-that-is and gold

If the wings of life grow weary
Let them rest within the cross
Of the circle in the spiral
And the silver-coated moss

For I'm bound to thee with sunshine
In the winter's wicked wind
That is fashioned in a pattern
Before it's ever pinned.

The Beautiful Cloud-hopper

Once upon a time in a deep valley, just north of the Alps and above the clouds, a Cloud-hopper felt the gentle breezes she knew as change. These clouds of change were sometimes moving briskly and brought with them some heavy weather. The Cloud-hopper knew to cover up and stay warm and dry within her frame of existence. She was a knower of truths, and this understanding of staying warm was beyond all thought for her. It was a deep understanding she could not explain nor cared to try.

The apprehension she carried about others not knowing to cover up and stay warm and dry was another matter. The Cloud-hopper was a mother of many, many mothers, and her desire to mother was so strong, that in order to let go of this old holding, of needing to mother so strongly, she made a deep decision to create a distance between those she mothered and herself. She did this in so many ways. It was time for her to change direction now and to receive mothering from herself. It was time for her to direct her heart-felt mothering towards her own soul-self, and so she did.

In a worldly view, this may look like chaos at times, yet it is not. It is a simple soul-decision to receive self-love and in doing so, be able to deeply ground your mothering capability in your own deeply felt experience of allowing yourself to be universally mothered by the mother of all living love, mother earth.

Now, let me get back to my storyline: As time went on, the Cloud-hopper had a deeper understanding of the beautiful path she walked upon. She began to see the flowers growing along this beautiful path she had chosen. They were not the flowers she had expected. They were the flowers of her dreams. She was on the road to full recovery of her selfhood. She knew instinctively which way she needed to walk, and step by step, she walked her walk so that step by step she could talk her talk. Soon she began to trust her process, and it wasn't long before her partner saw exactly how her new pattern was going. He settled into the new pattern and easily resonated with it. Together they had created a new, harmonious way to be more than they had been before, and so they *saw all is well.*

This was no small achievement for a Cloud-hopper from the Alps!

Self ID

In the woods of my imagining lives a sage that I call my own. He is a wise one of the wholeness continuum. He is not a ghost of himself trying to portray a fullness of life. He is the gentleness of every flower. He is the soft brightness of a warm day in May. He has a scepter at his side, which represents his self-authority and self-design. He knows his patterns. He accepts them all. He belongs to the wholeness within all.

This sage is my individuated self. He is my soul-understanding of the depth of *all is well* that is carried forward of its own accord in every moment presenting here, in this physical focus. He is the lantern of my heart's lightness. He is the certainty of the stars that shine at night, no matter what. He is my inner, my outer view of life. He is the unique expression of the wholeness that resounds in all life. He is my inner song, singing itself throughout eternity. He is my true colours shining through. He is the one true blue note, singing from the trumpet that I have fashioned from my own open flower. I know the note of this sage so well. It is the eternal song of life's hum, through me, with ease and grace. It is the resonance of now, together, whole and cohesive within the view of the glue that is my complete name—love-alone.

Inner Flight

In a thicket by the edge of a pond there lived a dragonfly. She was more beautiful than your heart could imagine. She was also a wise one. For so many, many years she had lived in the thicket on the pond's edge. She held a deep fear of flying. This is very unusual for a dragonfly. For this dragonfly, it is what she had chosen for herself as an experience. She had experienced much pain in her life because of her life decision. The pain is in the background now, as this dragonfly is seeing her potential to be free of the dark thicket she has hidden in.

In the beginning of this new phase or segment of the dragonfly's life, she was cautious and hesitant about stepping out of the thicket and looking around. She felt uncertain about her wings supporting her. She had experienced difficulties with them, and she could not see the larger, more powerful aspect of her wings beyond physical sight. She would step out of the thicket, feel the fear of not feeling supported and hide in the thicket once again.

One day in the fall of the year, the dragonfly made a deep decision to do what she really wanted to do. She contemplated this for some time. She gathered data from her environment by feeling vibrations that made her heart sing. Her energetic wings became stronger and stronger. Through feeling the fullness of her wings and the safety of them, she felt full of light and love. She felt first hand where her joyful sense of wherewithal came from. She stayed with herself wherever she went and became her own best friend.

The night bird in the thicket called to the dragonfly, saying, "All is well, child. All is well. You know exactly what you are wanting, and when you trust your heart's desire, it comes to you with mathematical exactitude." The dragonfly did not know about the night bird's nest in the thicket, and she was surprised at its voice. It was such a beautiful, soft voice that she did not feel afraid. She wondered about this fearless part of her being.

The night bird said, "This is your own inner voice calling to you, speaking in the soft frequencies that your heart alone can hear. You are now speaking softly enough to your heart-song, for it to take flight.

"Soon you will fly, dragonfly. Have no fear. The time is near. It is not a domestic flight. It is a flight of the soul. The ancestors are calling you home to your own true heart and you will soon know your innate capability to fly. Try, dragonfly, try. In the trying experience, the allowing of self arrives as if by magic."

The Brotherhood and Sisterhood of Light

Thank you, brother," a sister said as her brother left her side to travel further without her. He had been her guide of sorts for so long, she could not remember when their journeying together began. He was a warrior. She was a warrior, too, but in this lifetime, she had chosen to be a peaceful warrior and had left all of her weaponry behind, except for the light and love that is her power in every moment. She waited, watching him, as he walked away. His form was so familiar to her. His manner and his subtle movement brought comfort to her heart. She was heart-smart now. She saw the light in all things. She knew the source of all was this inner light of love, no matter the conditions presenting. She knew this eternal love pervaded all. She knew there was no place you could put your finger where this effulgent love-light was not.

A steady din filled her ears. It was the sound of time passing, and yet it was the sound of silence, too. Together, these two opposites, noise and silence, created a resonance of peace. She stood within this peace-filled middle space and came to know the parts and pieces of herself that she had refused to accept. Leo the lion-hearted was the biggest of these pieces, and he came in with all of his natural curiosity and certainty of movement to help her remember the strength of her heart, for this is what she had truly forgotten. She had forgotten the absolute strength of her unsheathed heart.

Standing beside her brother all of these years, she felt confident in his potential. Now it was time for her to discover her own power and to see that her power was undoubtedly the power of her unfettered heart. It was always her power, but she needed to recognize this in her heart to realize it fully. Self-realization is a funny thing. It is way beyond words. There are no plan layouts with steps A, B, C and D. It is simply a clear and certain intention to fully love yourself first and to honour the childlike being within your heart into full expression of all love's light that simply is fullness of life.

Her brother didn't seem to notice that she was gone from beside him. He had his own unique lessons to learn. He was focused on where he was going. He knew he needed to go from this place of self-denial, but he didn't know how. He just moved where he thought he needed to go. He had a little fear of feeling. Feeling was not his friend. He had been hurt by feeling, or so he thought. He went where he needed to go to soothe this ache in his gut that said, "Not enough, not enough."

Then one day, on the eve of his birthday, he saw himself differently. It was as if a bright light came on in his corner of the world, and he saw what was what. He saw himself as a part of the beauty he was in, and it changed his view. He came to realize that all things happen for a reason. He knew the light shone in his life, too, and for the first time in a very long time, he felt grateful to be alive. He felt grateful for the life in him, the life he had been honoured with. He sat on the side of his bed and gave thanks for his journey in this world. He saw the beauty of every passage he had passed through and every battle he had fought. He saw the love that was always with him and he saw, with compassion, the love he had refused to accept for himself. He wept for himself and let go of the judgments he had harboured against his own soul. He felt lighter and less edgy. He felt a part of living. He felt in the swim again. He walked with a lighter step and held his head up high. All of a sudden, he was enjoying his journey. He clearly saw that. He took it in. He laughed out loud at himself. "How could I have missed this beautiful simplicity?" he asked himself. "How?"

The rain beating on the metal roof jarred him out of his dreamy state and back into the bedroom. He looked around. He reached out and touched his face. "Yep, it's me!" he said. "I am alive and able to feel. Feeling is a gift. I am so thankful for feeling!"

The Jaguar

High in the Andes Mountains, jaguar sleeps. He is full to the gills and sleep overtakes him like a soft, easy cloud of peace pervading his entire being. He had run, jumped and sweated to catch a gazelle and now it was time to rest and relax in sleepy solitude, safe in his cave of darkness. The Spanish half of him wanted to dance, while the British side of him wanted to sing. He was so contented in his slumber, he let go of both halves and surrendered to whole relaxation, whole dreaming and whole presentation.

The night passed, uninterrupted, and at morning's first light, jaguar stirred from his deep contentment to see a smiling blue bird perched at his door. He had never seen a blue bird in these parts, let alone a smiling blue bird, and he asked the question, "Who are you and what have you come to say?"

"I've come for a day," said the blue bird. "I ask you to pray with me for all of humanity on the eventide of this long-awaited change."

The jaguar looked puzzled and looked all around him to check for changes in the view.

"It all looks the same!" he said, curiously. "Tell me what you mean."

The little blue bird began, in verse:

> There is a legend of long ago
> That is neither high nor low
> It is a tale of come and go
> And all that lies within the flow
> It's not held within a book
> And doesn't depend upon your look
> You'll see it where the blue birds fly
> You'll see it with your inner eye
> It is a tale just like your own

It is about the skills you hone
It's all about your inner light
And tells you there's no need to fight
The grass, the trees and flowers, too
All know the endless more of you
The time has come to see the sign
The time has come to walk the line
I am a bringer of my song
A song so true, a blue, blue throng
I'll sit and hum, so you can see
The beauty, breadth and depth of me
I am the cradle yet to be
I am the ashes you will see
I am the beast upon the hill
I am the baby sleeping still
I love the light of every day
I've come to show you this fine day
A day of peace that you can use
A day of peace that you can choose
And so the jaguar sat right up
He started drinking from the cup
The blue bird was fulfilled that day
The blue bird taught him how to pray
You see your daily needs are met
You take all needs from in the net
The vibrant song that you now hear
Is always close, is ever near
The jaguar roamed throughout the land
To share the love at his command
A truer blue did never speak
As from this loving blue bird's beak.

The Onion

Onions share a lesson with all survivors of the onslaught. Tears well up and the onion says, "It is just another layer, my dear. It is just another shadow moving past the sun to find out it was never a shadow to begin with, but a facet of a façade that no one recognized as truth. It became a stand-in for truth, and time marched on and truth was forgotten."

The onion, however, remained to tell its sad tale of love lost and misdeeds presenting. It shed skin after skin after blessed skin until it came to reside in the truth of its core, and there it found no more layers to peel off and no more welling up of fear.

In the core, the onion found its eternal wellness, and this well was dry. It was the wind of change blowing through every lost love and every seeming misdeed presenting. Here the onion stopped and surveyed the territory. "What the?" she asked.

Non-reaction presented itself as absolute love at the onion's core, and a chorus of love-alone reflected back the truth of the onion being the glory bee.

Endless Coil of Now

Here we are again, in the hallowed halls, together. *The divine blanket cloaks us and wisdom is our common mantra.*

"Blessings be!" said the bee
It's so great to be free
Back and forth from the hive
Filled with life, so alive

Honoured questions you gave
Can't take me to the grave
For indeed, with my eye
I see we do not die

Gentle men I have taught
That in life don't get caught
Listen to everything
And you won't feel the sting

Ghosts are nothing but show
They are not seed you sow
Open up every door
Open to Evermore

In the past we forget
Our life's not over yet
We forget the Great Coil
This is truly our soil.

The Hobbit on the Hill

There was a farmer who had many, many geese. He loved every one of them deeply. He would forfeit none of them to the winds that blow strongly upon this earth. The farmer tended to each goose exactly as it required tending, and he kept his gaggle together wherever he went. He was the talk of the town. He was known as the Hobbit on the Hill.

In early December, a strong north wind blew through the village, and with it came a raging blizzard that froze half of the Hobbit's flock. The sacrifices he made to save the geese nearly killed him, and he became very ill for a long while.

During this time and space, a crown appeared on the Hobbit's head, and on the crown could be seen a brilliant light. This light was so bright, it shone from the Hobbit's hilltop for all to see. Townsfolk came from near and far to investigate the shining. As these folk gathered around the Hobbit, they not only saw the light, but they fully felt it, too. They all came together in this light to assist the Hobbit and his remaining flock to health again.

In the spring, the Hobbit was well and so were his geese. He had created an invisible bridge from beyond for all to more clearly see the beauty of life. If ever the townsfolk felt blue or alone, they only had to look up to the light on the hill and remember the love they felt in the *Great Coming Together,* as they called it, and their wellbeing was restored.

In the end, the Hobbit passed on and the townsfolk shared the tending of his flock. His light remained on the hill, although nobody knew exactly how this was. Through the ages, the story of the Hobbit and his light was passed down, and on a dark night, if you are very still and look up above the tallest hill, you may see a bright light. If you enter into it, you will feel it, too.

Samuel Read

Samuel Read was a writer
A lover of kith and of kin
Samuel Read was a biter
He'd latch on and never give in

Samuel lived to love graces
He loved all the ebb and the flow
He was the writer of faces
A gleaner of seeds he would sow

Samuel lived on a pig farm
He loved every squeal and each oink
Living the life of complete charm
Until, on his head he got boinked

A seedpod as big as a suitcase
Came crashing right down on his crown
Samuel squirrel, a seed-ace,
Found this seed a trial to own

He laid himself out on a tree branch
The tree trunk went twirling around
Then Samuel, in a slight trance
Found himself down on the ground

The moral or midst of this story
Is sometimes a struggle to find
Remember the love and the glory
While saying farewell to the mind.

The Balance Beam of Now

"Irresponsible—who said I was irresponsible?? What are you talking about? I am, too, responsible if you ask me, but of course, nobody's asking me!"

The balance-beam of the middle-way is a hard one to walk at times, but we learn so much about our capable soul by doing this. We fall off to the left, we fall off to the right and we get back on and learn, slowly, slowly, not to fall off at all but to remain fully with ourselves under all types of circumstances, and soon it becomes easy to remain fully present for others, too, and not fall off the beam.

This beam is the beam of white light that is our true connection with all that is. Some call it the silver thread of connection to all. To honour yourself, you need to know yourself deeply and love the uniqueness of your pattern and design. One would not say that a pattern was wrong or right. When we quit grasping for pleasure and stop avoiding pain in the process, we see that all of our living is beautiful. Natural emissaries of light, in unlimited forms, show up to guide and encourage us because we accept they can.

The road gets easier, and then there is no road. There are just connections—endless connections to exactly what is known, and off we go to discover the threads of a new lesson of light, without grasping or aversion, but joyful encounter. We just go with the flow of love that guides our heart and start to know the steady flow that beckons all life forward as a sense of what works or fits or settles us in a way our mind cannot quite fully comprehend. We are on our way to self-love and thus, love of all life. This is the universal free-way.

Often a call on love can lead us down a beautiful garden path that we did not even know existed, except in our imagination. Let the good times flow and know for certain that love is all there really is, everywhere. The rest is trite.

Living Well

A joyful voice has found me now
I know not why, I know not how
I bow my head and take a breath
I know I have no fear of death

A bringer of the dawn, with all
Together, we will all walk tall
To carry light within our heart
To stand so still and play our part

A seed of golden light appears
I recognize it through the years
I call its name, it answers clear
I know that love is very near

Recompense, I thought I knew
Will teach me deeply of the stew
The flavour in the central part
Reveals a lifelong work of art

A vision quest, within, to find
The magic I had left behind
With joyful voice I rise to say
Thank you, Life, for this fine day.

Heart Notes

Heart Notes